OREGON RIVER TOURS

by
JOHN GARREN

New edition

Including 23 river tours

A guide to Oregon's most popular whitewater rivers.

Garren Publishing
01008 S.W. Comus
Portland, OR 97219

**To
Patrick E. Murphy**

Oregon River Tours, Copyright © 1991
      by John H. Garren
Printed in the United States of America
ISBN No. 0-941887-01-4
Library of Congress Catalog Number 90-82898
New Edition published January 1991
Second printing October 1992
Third printing January 1996

Cover photos: Front: Jeff Garren — Deschutes River
                  Back: Jon S. Garren — Deschutes River

CONTENTS

Acknowledgment

In preparing river logs for the first edition of **Oregon River Tours**, it became evident that logging is a two person job. Trying to log rivers in a kayak is particularly frustrating. Virtually all the river tours were logged in a raft using two persons. The second person in this duo is Mary Alice Thompson. She handles trip logistics, meals, a Volkswagen bus and provides the trip log on all raft trips.

Mary Alice is a competent river person in her own right. She has a knowledge of river hydraulics that surpasses most boat persons and can confidently run class four rivers, except possibly at high discharge where strength rather than skill might be a factor. She is clearly the outfitter for these tours and a major contributor to the book.

Jon S. Garren and Jeff Garren are excellent paddlers and boating companions. They shared these trips by helping with photography and the routine chores inherent with any river trip. Most important they have a sense for guiding and safety. They are river wise in everything from dislocated shoulders to class five rapids. I can think of no two better paddlers to have around.

Foreword

"Those people left us and crossed the (Columbia) river through the highest waves I ever saw a small vestles ride. Those Indians are certainly the best canoe navigators I ever saw."

The Journals of Lewis and Clark
Monday, November 11th 1805.

Oregonians have a long history as boaters. Our extensive system of rivers and Oregonian's love of the outdoors have naturally drawn many to our rivers for fishing, camping, boating and recreating in an environment that lends itself to an enviable quality of life. Oregon has 35,000 miles of named rivers. There is an historical record of over 165 rivers having modern day boating use. Indeed virtually all Oregon rivers are boated. Oregon's entire coastal waters are free with open access to the public. Also our State Constitution guarantees that all navigable rivers shall be, without toll, open waterway transportation corridors for the public.

The Rogue River is a charter river in the original 1968 Federal Wild and Scenic Rivers Act. By initiative petition Oregonians passed the 1969 State Scenic Waterways Act. Due to legislative inaction in designating new rivers in the system and the threat of wholesale damming of remaining free flowing rivers, the people again by initiative petition in 1988, gave protection to additional rivers. Also, in 1988 the Federal Omnibus Oregon Wild and Scenic Rivers Act was sponsored by Senator Hatfield with endorsement by five of the six Oregon Congressional delegates. The passage of this bill gave protection under the Federal Wild and Scenic Rivers Act to over forty new federally designated river sections in Oregon. For the first twenty years of the Federal Act and nineteen years of the State Act there was negligible success in protecting rivers under either legislation. Suddenly, in 1988, Oregon became the national leader in river protection.

Today Oregon has 26 river sections totalling 1,167 miles, included in the State Scenic Waterways Act and 47 river sections totalling 1,677 miles protected by the Federal Wild and Scenic Rivers legislation. The Northwest Power Planning Council proposes that 15,000 miles of Oregon rivers be protected from dams and adverse development in order to enhance fisheries and to protect the large public investment in that resource. There can be no question that Oregonians feel strongly about one of the state's greatest resources —free flowing rivers.

Oregon River Tours was first published in 1973. Prior to that time there were no Oregon river guide books though many Oregon rivers had been explored and boated. The major expansion of whitewater boating came after the 1968 and 1969 Federal and State legislation concerning rivers. Shortly after 1973 new federal regulations and management practices on rivers such as the Rogue and Snake caused what people term the "boating explosion". At first the main increase on these limited access rivers was commercial tourism responding to a newly created exclusive market, but private boater use also expanded, until now private boaters far exceed commercial tourists in spite of national advertising for the latter.

As use increased, a new and better informed river user constituency developed that had not previously existed. Today's Oregon boaters are aware of river issues such as the effect of low-head hydro projects, the charging of a toll for the use of the Deschutes River and the controversial system of allocation of boating access on the federally regulated Rogue and Snake rivers. Oregon boaters are concerned with, and influence the outcome of, such things as river initiative petitions and river management.

Following the State and Federal designations of newly protected rivers in 1988, over forty river management plans have been completed. By 1996 most of the required plans will be ready for implementation. Boaters should check rivers they boat annually for information regarding new regulations. The Deschutes, for example, will be Oregon's third limited access river requiring permits on certain days and passes on the remainder. Fire restrictions, carry out of human waste and camp assignments are regulations being considered on some rivers where these regulations are not presently required.

In the first 1973 edition, when whitewater boating was just beginning to expand, **Oregon River Tours** contained thirteen tours. Each printing has added to and revised the content as the whitewater era unfolded. This sixth and latest edition is no exception, as rivers are added reflecting recent additions of the 1988 State and Federal river legislation. Today's boaters have superior equipment, high skills and routinely boat rivers that in 1973 were considered hazardous. **Oregon River Tours** has attempted to keep pace with the dramatic increase in whitewater boating. The result is a guide to the most popular whitewater tours in Oregon.

4

OREGON RIVER TOURS

			Page				Page
①	②	Clackamas	21		⑬	Metolius	153
③	④	Deschutes	31		⑭	Minam	163
	⑤	Grande Ronde	57		⑮	Molalla	171
	⑥	Hood	69	⑯	⑰	Owyhee	177
	⑦	Illinois	75		⑱	Rogue	207
⑧	⑨	John Day	95		⑲	Sandy	227
	⑩	John Day, North	127		⑳	Santiam, North	233
	⑪	Klamath	137		㉑	Santiam, South	241
	⑫	McKenzie	148		㉒	Snake	245
					㉓	Umpqua, North	263

Selecting the Tours

Most Oregon rivers are "young" rivers with headwaters originating in rugged mountains where river slopes are steep, stream roughness and hazards are high and stream discharges are low. From the headwaters these rivers flow through a transition zone, usually still within mountain areas, then into older more established valleys and finally into the Pacific Ocean. Most of the tours chosen for this book are in the transition zone, downstream from the headwaters and upstream from flatwater.

With over 35,000 miles of named rivers and 165 rivers with a historical record of being boated in Oregon, it is apparent that some criteria must be used to produce a practical river guide book. The river sections I chose are ones that I personally have boated, and that I would recommend to friends. Many other Oregon rivers are boatable, but did not meet the selection criteria for this type of book. In establishing the criteria I considered river flow, rapids difficulty, safety, access, boater popularity, length of tour and quality of wilderness experience. All the tours are intended for whitewater boaters.

The chosen river tours have sufficient water to boat for a period of time rather than only during brief periods at flood stage. The rapids difficulty ranges between class 2 and 4 with an occasional class 5 rapids if a practical portage of that rapids is available. Ease of access and length of tour were considered to avoid such inconveniences as long driving periods for short boating sections and complicated launches or take outs. The length of tours selected is approximately 15 miles for day trips and at least 30 miles for possible overnight trips. Preference was given to overnight trips with a high quality of wilderness experience. Of the twenty-three tours, twelve are day trips and eleven are overnight trips. Evaluation based on these criteria resulted in tours ranging from class 2 rapids difficulty for intermediate boaters to tours including class 4 or 5 rapids requiring expert boating skills.

River Tour Data

Number	River	Section	Trip Length Miles	Average Slope Ft./Mi.	Recommended Discharge Gage	* Maximum Rapids Difficulty
1	Clackamas, Upper	Sandstone Bridge Big Cliff	14	34	1,000-5,000 Three Lynx	4
2	Clackamas, Lower	Lower McIver Park Mouth	20	13	1,500-5,000 Estacada	2
3	Deschutes, Upper	Highway 26 Sherars Bridge	54	13	4,000-7,000 Moody	4
4	Deschutes, Lower	Lone Pine Mouth	40	12	4,000-7,000 Moody	3
5	Grande Ronde	Minam Troy	46	21	2,000-5,000 Troy	2
6	Hood	Dee Tucker Bridge	8	64	5.0 gage Tucker Bridge	4
7	Illinois	Miami Bar Oak Flat	32	23	800-2,500 Kerby	5
8	John Day, Upper	Service Creek Clarno	49	8	2,000-6,000 Service Creek	2
9	John Day, Lower	Clarno Cottonwood Bridge	69	11	2,000-6,000 Service Creek	3
10	John Day, North	Camas Creek Monument	40	18	2,000-5,000 Monument	2
11	Klamath	Boyle Powerhouse Copco Lake	17	49	1,600 Boyle Powerhouse	5
12	McKenzie	Blue River Leaburg Dam	18	16	1,500-5,000 Vida	3
13	Metolius	Lower 99 Bridge Camp Monty	17	43	1,500 Near Grandview	3
14	Minam	Minam Lodge Mouth	22	48	1,000-2,000 Minam	3
15	Molalla	Bridge-Mile 35 Feyrer Park	14	35	3.0-4.5 feet Feyrer Bridge	3
16	Owyhee, Middle	Three Forks Rome	35	17	1,000-3,000 Rome	(Portage) 5 (6)
17	Owyhee, Lower	Rome Leslie Gulch	10 miles on reservoir 62	to reservoir 14	1,000-4,000 Rome	3
18	Rogue	Graves Creek Foster Bar	35	13	1,500-4,000 Agness	(Portage) 4 (5)
19	Sandy	Dodge Park Dabney Park	13	13	1,500-4,000 Bull Run	3
20	Santiam, North	Packsaddle Park Mehama	16	23	1,500-4,000 Big Cliff Dam	3
21	Santiam, South	Foster Dam Waterloo Park	14	11	1,000-4,000 Foster Dam	2
22	Snake	Hells Canyon Dam Grande Ronde River	79	10	10,000-15,000 Hells Canyon Dam	5
23	Umpqua, North	Boulder Flat Camp Gravel Bin	14	32	1,000-2,000 Copeland Creek	4

* See log for discharge at which rapids were rated.

River Data

The intent of this book is to provide useful information primarily for the boater using these river tours for the first time or those who may use the river only infrequently. Each tour includes a river map, a trip narrative, a river discharge curve and a river log with campsites and rapids.

Essentially this is a river log for the person who will actually boat the river. The log is believed to be unique because it is a graphical log including both time and distance.

In preparing the river tours, a certain research technique and river data gathering method was necessary. The most important data is discussed for the boater's information.

River Slope

River slope is usually measured by boaters in feet of river drop per mile. This data can roughly be scaled from conventional U.S. Geological Survey Contour Maps, obtained from river-mile index publications, or more accurately from river profile maps. By looking at the profile you can tell whether a river has a relatively constant slope or is what boaters call a "pool and drop" river. The latter will have more rapids which form at each "drop" section. The river slope is one measure of river difficulty. Steep river slopes will have high river velocity and will usually, but not necessarily, have difficult rapids. The river slope given in the log is for the trip average. This is an indicator of river difficulty, but other factors must be considered when evaluating the river. When river profiles are available, it is good practice to review them in making an evaluation of river difficulty.

River Roughness

River roughness greatly influences river difficulty. The rocky "rough" stream channel provides the basis for a wide variety of stream hydraulics that form rapids. Hydrologists can determine numerical values for stream roughness, but a minimum of common sense experience quickly tells the boater whether the river is rough or smooth.

A relatively uniform stream slope and smooth channel usually provide easy river boating. A rough channel combined with certain river slope and discharge often ends up with a name like Blossom, Green Wall, White Horse and Wild Sheep rapids.

River Discharge

River discharge is one of the most important factors to be considered by the boater. There is a relatively narrow range of discharge which gives desirable boating for any river. Below some minimum discharge the stream velocity decreases, the stream roughness (rocks) becomes troublesome and the trip is difficult. The other end of the range is flood stage with high velocity and powerful hydraulic forces. Desirability depends on the individual boater; some boaters prefer low discharge and others seek the challenge of big water at flood stage.

The river hydrographs shown with each tour tell the boater at what times certain discharges may be expected. The graphs show mean monthly flows at a specific gage location and are for a historical period of record. The graphs can be used to predict peak run-off periods and for river trip planning. An estimate can be made of the time and magnitude of low, moderate or high flows. Actual flows may be obtained from the National Weather Service at trip time. River flows are usually given in cubic feet per second since gage heights have meaning only to boaters familiar with a specific gage.

Most of these tours have either a mean annual discharge or a maximum mean monthly discharge exceeding 1,000 c.f.s. Rivers with smaller flows can usually be boated only during brief periods at flood stage.

Oregon is a marine west coast climate where the water year begins in October. The maritime climate produces maximum precipitation during the winter months. At lower elevations this is rain with peak river runoff in December or January. For rivers with a significant area of the drainage basin as high elevation, the winter precipitation is in the form of snow, storing water for a peak runoff in May as warm weather approaches. By summer many of the natural flowing rivers are too low to boat. Thus elevation of the drainage basin distinguishes between what boaters refer to as "rain" or "snow" rivers.

The Cascade mountain range forms the geographical border between types of rivers. Most of the rivers west of the Cascades are rain rivers and those east are snow rivers. The river hydrograph is an indicator of river type.

Estimating Time of River Discharge

The river log gives recommended ranges of discharge for drift boating. These are general boating guidelines based on experience and judgment. Boating at discharges outside this range is tolerable under certain conditions, and the experienced boater realizes the lower discharges mean slow velocity along with rock problems. The top range of discharge means more powerful river hydraulics close to flood stage.

Usually it is desirable for the boater to schedule trips for the most probable boating periods between selected ranges of discharge. As an aid in predicting river discharge time, river gages were selected for analysis that typically represent river conditions. Sample data was plotted for the mean monthly discharge over a discrete period of record. The resulting data gives a smooth graph based on past river history.

Plotting the mean values gives a more useful graph than those based on one year's data. These graphs prepared for each river are considered sufficiently accurate for all long-range planning. As the trip approaches the boater should verify reality by calling the National Weather Service for exact data and short-term predictions of less than one month. These curves are practical means of estimating what periods of the year are normally used for boating within a selected range of discharges.

The National Weather Service in Portland recently changed its phone number to (503) 261-9246. A recording gives river gage height for West Coast Basin rivers (Nehalem, Wilson, Nestucca, Siletz, Alsea, Siuslaw), and river flows in c.f.s. for the Willamette River Drainage (Clackamas at Three Lynx, Clackamas at Estacada, Sandy at Bull Run, North Santiam at Mehama, South Santiam at Waterloo, McKenzie at Vida), Southwest Drainage (Rogue at Agness, Illinois at Kerby, North Umpqua at Winchester), and Eastern Drainage (Owyhee at Rome, Grande Ronde at Troy, John Day at Service Creek, Hood at Tucker Bridge, Deschutes at Moody). With the exception of the North Umpqua River, the river gages used in the recording are the same as those in Oregon River Tours. The Copeland Creek gage on the North Umpqua is not available to the National Weather Service for daily readings. The recording changes during the year, dependent on river use and flows.

The River Log

The river log is the heart of each tour. Although boaters experienced in running a particular river often do not use a log, it is considered essential for boaters running a river for the first time. Rivers were logged by time which is then correlated with map data, river mile indexes and other information that can be confirmed.

In this publication of Oregon River Tours, the log consists of a map with time and rapids of class three or greater difficulty and sometimes class two rapids. This is generally sufficient information for boaters on the shorter day trips. On some longer overnight tours a straight line time log is also included with the map. This is an additional aid to show in greater detail the river characteristics along with camps for trip planning. Some boaters prefer a straight line time log for navigating while others are map oriented. Where appropriate, both are given. For the most part everything on the logs can be seen by the boater. The exceptions are airstrips, some ranches or points of interest. The boater may want to know where these features are for emergencies or for hiking. By following either the map or the straight line log the boater should be able to locate rapids and camps on the tours.

Distance and Time

Distance is a difficult concept for most people while on the river. A new boater can get lost unless he has some check points as a reference. This is why time in addition to distance is included in the log. To say that the next major rapids is downstream 7.3 miles has little meaning, unless it is related to something familiar such as time. I have checked the logs frequently and find the time very accurate under similar conditions. When the times do vary, it is easy to re-set your watch at some convenient check point and get back on schedule. It is easy to keep track of both real and river time with a watch that has a stop watch function.

The main concerns of most boaters are major rapids and camps. These are specially pointed out in the log. Generally, the boater should be prepared to scout and possibly portage major rapids.

River Mileage

River mileage conventionally starts at the mouth and increases upstream. Left or right bank is facing downstream. All the river logs use this convention.

Relative Drift Time

The relative drift time for various boats is significantly different. Log times are recorded for a particular type boat at a particular river stage. For the same type boat and reasonably similar river stage there is little difference in time. For example, it will usually not be necessary to correct times, except at check points, for canoes or kayaks, but if you are using a raft and the log time is for a canoe, you may expect the raft drift time to be longer by a direct ratio of 1.6/1.1 or about 1.5. Multiply the canoe log times by this amount and correct the log times before starting the trip. You should then come very close to actual times, and correct only at convenient check points.

The river log trip time is actual drift time on the river. When you stop or want to get out for awhile, note the time; then when you start again, set your watch back to the time you got out, and you are back on the correct log time.

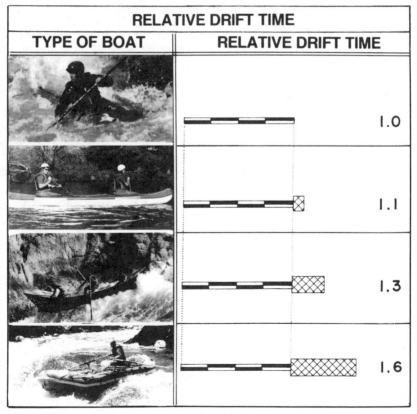

RELATIVE DRIFT TIME	
TYPE OF BOAT	**RELATIVE DRIFT TIME**
	1.0
	1.1
	1.3
	1.6

FIGURE 1

12

There will be some minor differences between individuals for rowing and paddling. The recorded log times are for drifting, which means paddling or rowing just to maintain position — or to maneuver with continuous but leisurely rowing or paddling in low velocity or slack-water areas. Log times might be cut in half in an all-out race, but the times are remarkably close for drifting.

River Velocity

One other main factor, in addition to type of boat, that influences drift time is river velocity. Within reasonable limits of river discharge from that shown in the log, it will be unnecessary to correct river drift time. If, however, the log is for 5,000 c.f.s. and you plan to boat at 2,000 c.f.s., it may be desirable to correct for the change in river velocity in addition to boat type.

Boaters are aware that as river discharge increases so does the river velocity. Yet even with the wide range of boats and river discharges used in these logs, there is a surprisingly narrow range of drift speeds, usually between 4 to 5 miles per hour for the trip average. Apparently as the river slows down boaters work harder at paddling, and as river velocity increases they maneuver and paddle approximately at river velocity.

Many boaters dislike a watch on river trips, yet it is essential if the boater is concerned about navigating on the river. I use time as a means of navigating in an attempt to estimate when river hazards will arrive, in locating camps and to avoid cooking in the dark or spending an unforeseen day on the river.

Example: The log you intend to use was prepared for a trip with an average river drop of 15 feet per mile, using a McKenzie drift boat and a river discharge of 5,000 cubic feet per second. You plan to use a raft at a river discharge of 2,000 cubic feet per second. From the Relative Drift Table (Figure 1) and Estimated River Velocity (Figure 2) graphs, estimate your drift time.

Time correction (boat type correction) (river velocity correction)

$$\left(\frac{1.6}{1.3}\right) \quad \left(\frac{4.5}{3.0}\right) \quad = \quad 1.8$$

It will take you about 1.8 times longer than the times shown in the log. This is a significant change, and you may wish to correct river log times to major rapids and special geographic check points before starting your trip.

ESTIMATED RIVER VELOCITY

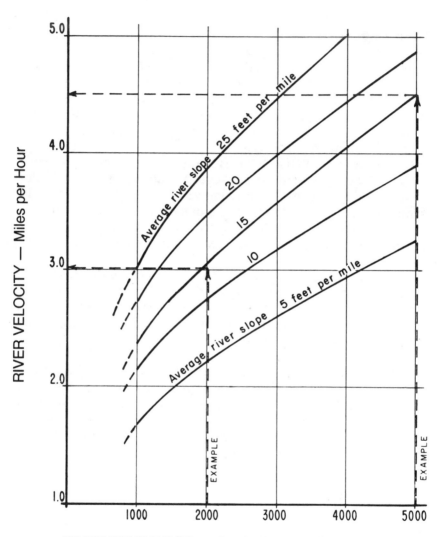

RIVER VELOCITY — Miles per Hour

RIVER DISCHARGE — Cubic Feet per Second

FIGURE 2

14

Campsites

Campsite lists are included on overnight river tours where an agency has published such a list. These camps are also shown on the river maps. Many of the camps have been established primarily by boater use over a period of time. Marginal camps are being established as river use increases, and agencies are in a continual process of camp alteration and designation.

Camps are listed primarily as a trip planning aid. On some rivers during heavy use periods camps can be at a premium. None of the Oregon rivers require campsite reservations. Most Oregon rivers are not limited access permit rivers, so camp reservations are impractical. As pressure on the rivers, and on the campsites, increases more careful planning is necessary to increase the odds of finding an adequate campsite at a reasonable time of day. Some boating groups have caused controversy by their use of lead boats and camp exchanges or bogus camps to reserve spots for their parties.

River Maps

Each tour has a map that shows the launch and the take out. In addition, camps are shown on overnight trips and, depending on the character of the trip, class 3 or greater rapids. River miles are included in the time log for navigating. This data along with checkpoints such as bridges or sidestreams, combines on one sheet all the pertinent information a boater usually needs. The maps are from the boaters point of view and most things show on the maps can be seen by the boater. Contours and routine geography tend to blur on the river and are not shown.

The river flow on all maps is from the bottom of the page toward the top. This is consistent with the river bank convention where left and right bank corresponds to left and right sides of the map facing downstream.

The only other map needed is a state highway map to get to the launch and for planning the shuttle. Small communities and named places such as Troy, Minam, Twickenham, Clarno and Rome are shown on the highway map. The general location of each tour is shown on the map in the front of the book.

For most day trips the river and vicinity map show sufficient detail to plan the shuttle. On some of the overnight trips a schematic shuttle map is included as an aid in shuttle planning. By using a state highway map, in conjunction with the maps in Oregon River Tours, the boater should easily be able to find the launch, take out, and plan the shuttle.

Map Legend

 River mile

Camp

● 4 Rapids difficulty

Bridge

〜〜 Sidestream

Airstrip

Building

Spring

Boat launch

Elevation River elevation

Federal, state,
Forest Service road numbers

River Safety

River running is a risk sport, but contrary to popular belief, actual whitewater fatalities are surprisingly low. Reducing accidents or fatalities to a common denominator, such as drownings per 100,000 user days, the risk falls below other more accepted sports. Sometimes water related accidents are not, in fact, whitewater accidents, and agency reporting methods may account for some of the discrepancy in facts. In any event rational people who boat whitewater attempt to reduce risk to the lowest practical level.

In order to advance skills and experience challenge, many boaters, by preference, boat near their skill limits. Logic might suggest that the majority of whitewater fatalities are poorly equipped beginners without any skill or judgement. There are no statistics to bear this out, and the risks of the novice boating Class 2 rapids may be very close to the risks of the expert boater attempting Class 5 rapids. Some boaters, by choice, are willing to accept greater risks than others. There is no criteria to determine whether beginners or experts are greater risk takers. There is a tendency to forget that all boaters were at one time beginners. If there are more accidents among beginning boaters than experts, it is probably because there are so many more of them.

The three primary factors influencing safety are equipment, skills and judgement. The boater has the control of, and responsibility for, each of these factors. No person, agency, certification or set of regulations can relieve the boater from the responsibility. The individual must make the decision whether his skills and the particular circumstances warrant running a river or rapids.

A high level of river skills and judgement only come from experience. This experience develops people who are worth seeking out as boating companions since companions are the only persons available for rescue and help in case of an emergency on the river. The river has a way of weeding out the frivolous who are unwilling or unable to develop the skills and judgement required of whitewater boating. River safety is strictly up to the individual and his immediate boating companions.

Rapids Difficulty Classification

Whitewater rapids are formed by river hydraulics from a combination of slope, stream roughness and flow. The most used and best understood method of classifying rapids is the international system based on a scale of 1 through 6 where 1 is the easiest and 6 the most difficult. Experienced river runners have classified major rapids on many popular river runs. The classifiers have developed a consensus on rating, and seldom will experienced boaters differ by one whole classification number.

The primary differences that occasionally exist in rapids classification often relate to confusing rapids difficulty classifications with boater skills. Although the two are related, rapids difficulty classification for a specific set of conditions is constant and independent of river or location. Boater skills and perception of rapids are constantly changing. Rivers are routinely being run today that were considered hazardous ten years ago. In most cases it isn't the rapids that have changed but rather the equipment, skills and attitudes of the boater. The boater has the responsibility to confirm rapids classifications for himself, since it is the boater who will ultimately run these rapids. It must be emphasized that any rapids rating must also be associated with a river flow since rapids may change with flow.

To distinguish between rapids class and boater skills, it is best to use the numerical classification for rapids and an adjective for skills such as novice, intermediate or expert. Environmental conditions such as temperature, remoteness or ease of rescue may influence the judgement used in running a river, but these factors are independent of the rapids classification.

The western rapids classifications system has been used on some of the southwestern rivers. The original scale was 10 with 10+ and 10++. This is double the international scale, making conversions between western and international scales easy. Other methods of

17

rapids classification have been proposed, but they have not received any preference over the international classification by the boating community.

Different organizations have also used descriptions for each numerical classification. Many of these are lengthy and often reflect regionalization or a particular boating background. A simpler method that does not change the classification scale refers each classification to whitewater hazard varying from virtually no hazard to extreme hazard. The threshold of hazard for most boaters is class 3. Obviously, boaters can have accidents in class 1 rapids or no rapids at all but in terms of whitewater, hazards increase with the numerical classification.

Ordinarily river logs and maps only show class 3 and greater rapids and named class 2 rapids. Some class 2 rapids are shown where they add to clarity in showing river difficulty.

International Rapids Difficulty Class	Whitewater Hazard	Boater Skill
1	Virtually None	Beginner
2	Hardly Any	Novice
3	Threshold of Hazard	Intermediate
4	Moderate	Expert
5	High	Advanced Expert
6	Substantial Hazard to Life	None

Drinking Water

In the past it was common practice for boaters to drink water directly from clear rivers and sidestreams. For the past several years there have been numerous problems with that troublesome protozoa, Lambia Giardia, and other river pollutants. Anyone who has ever experienced a full-blown case of "giardia" will be a true believer in treating all drinking or cooking water and paying special attention to personal and camp sanitation. The boaters equivalent of "Montezuma's Revenge" has an incubation period of about 18 days so that the only good thing is that the boater probably won't experience it on the river trip where it was contracted.

Suffice it to say that all water on all of these tours should be treated. Boiling is the simplest solution or using one of the better water purification filters.

Car Shuttling

Vehicle shuttling is one trip planning consideration common to all boaters. Most boaters who do not have the time to perform their own shuttle prefer to hire people in the area who make a business of shuttling. Shuttle driving is inherently seasonal and can involve transients with no responsibility or liability.

It makes sense that before entrusting your vehicle to a shuttle service and paying them a handsome sum, some inquiry should be made about their reliability. The vehicle should be parked in a supervised area during the boating trip and delivered within a few hours of the take-out, with the drivers preferably meeting the boaters. Leaving a vehicle overnight in an unattended transfer area, launch or take-out point is inviting vandalism.

Usually the river managing agency will provide a list of shuttle services on request. The list changes constantly, and since these services are not under agency permit, there is no implied responsibility. The references in this book are not all inclusive, but most have been referred by the agencies and used successfully.

Class V Shuttle

Clackamas River, The Narrows — R.M. 45

Upper Clackamas River

Sandstone Bridge to Big Cliff

The Clackamas River begins near the summit of the Cascade Mountains in a series of lakes in the shadow of Olallie Butte. It flows northwesterly over 83 miles to its confluence with the Willamette River near Oregon City. The lakes source has an elevation of 5,000 feet, and the confluence at Oregon City has an elevation of 20 feet. While the Clackamas River is considered mainly a rain river, the high elevation of its source means that snow can have a major influence on run-off. A combination of rain and snow melt on December 22, 1964, swelled the Clackamas to a discharge of 120,000 c.f.s. at its mouth and 68,200 c.f.s. at the Three Lynx gaging station at river mile 47.8. Boaters use the Three Lynx gaging station as a reference for flows in the Upper Clackamas river sections.

The Upper Clackamas has been defined as those waters above backwaters of the North Fork Reservoir beginning at river mile 35. The Lower Clackamas is that section of the river downstream from River Mill Dam near McIver Park at river mile 23.3. In between the upper and lower sections is a series of hydroelectric projects that offer reservoir boating except for a short, seldom run stretch of whitewater during periodic releases below the Cazadero diversion dam at river mile 28.

There are several sections in addition to the section described in this log that are run by boaters. Limited boating is done on the Oak Grove Fork of the Clackamas, the Austin Hot Springs section of the Clackamas, the Collowash and Fish Creek tributaries and the often referred to "killer fang" section of the Clackamas from the Collowash to Sandstone Bridge. These are potentially hazardous sections that should be run only in company with experienced boaters who know these sections. Recent logging on the Austin Hot Springs section, and logs and cables for fish habitat on the Fish Creek section, have introduced new hazards for boaters.

As a practical matter most boating is done within a 14 mile section from Sandstone Bridge (R.M. 48.5) to the log scaling station near Big Cliff (R.M. 35). One of the most frequently run sections, particularly by kayakers, is from Fish Creek to Bob's Hole. (R.M. 41.7 — R.M. 37.5 or road mile 36.5). Road mile markers are about one mile less than river miles. Bob's Hole is the site of the Annual Bob's Hole kayaking contest, and annual raft races are held in the vicinity of Carter Bridge (R.M. 40).

The section described in the river log used to be considered a difficult whitewater run. At low and moderate flows, it is now

21

routinely boated by thousands. Mostly it is class two whitewater with enough class three rapids, and Carters Bridge rapids which is class 4, to make the trip exciting. Only the "Headwall" rapids at river mile 42 has any significant history of fatalities and these have been grossly exaggerated depending on who is doing the story telling. In about 1980 kayakers put in a self rescue rope at the "Headwall" which was later replaced with a chain ladder. To my knowledge there hasn't been a fatality since. Unlucky boaters now climb out of the "Headwall", scramble about 300 yards up a steep slope to a trail and hike downstream two miles to the Fish Creek trailhead and bridge. Boaters often stop at the "Headwall" and check to see if the chain ladder is in place on their way to Sandstone Bridge or upriver launches.

Whitewater information with a map, rapids difficulty, class, names and a color-coded river level gage are at the Carter Bridge. Yellow on the gage is low or under 2,000 c.f.s. Green is moderate flows or 2,000 — 5,000 c.f.s. and high is red or over 5,000 c.f.s. The National Weather Service has recorded flow information for the Three Lynx gage during the main boating season.

Some of the rapids on this section have dual names. Powerhouse rapids at R.M. 48.5 is often called Three Lynx. Rock Garden rapids at R.M. 43 is also called Roaring River. The Headwall at R.M. 41.5 has been called Hole in the Wall and Toilet Bowl. The Crag at R.M. 39 below Carter Bridge is called Sling Shot by kayakers. Toilet Bowl at river mile 38 just below Big Eddy is sometimes called The Chute. With so many people using the river it is inevitable that individual descriptive names be given rapids. Perhaps the important thing is to know the difficulty classification and location of rapids rather than their names.

For boaters unfamiliar with the Upper Clackamas the following rapids are worth scouting. Most can be seen from the road or by taking a short walk. Three Lynx Powerhouse area at R.M. 48, The Narrows at R.M. 45, Roaring River (Rock Garden) at R.M. 44, The Headwall at R.M. 42, Carter Bridge at R.M. 40, Big Eddy at R.M. 39 and Toilet Bowl (The Chute) at R.M. 39.

The Upper Clackamas is "home" to over a million people in the greater Portland metropolitan area and Willamette Valley communities. The paralleling road makes this area easily accessible to campers, fishermen, hikers, boaters and log trucks. Except possibly during the summer low water, the river is boated essentially year around.

On any Sunday you can find the locals sharpening whitewater skills, practicing surfing, doing endos or freestyle at rapids such as Bob's Hole. There are play spots from Fish Creek to Bob's Hole at most any river stage between 800 c.f.s. and upwards. Flows between 2,300 — 2,900 c.f.s. are considered best for Bob's Hole.

The Clackamas River canyon is a green canyon of old growth Douglas Fir shrouded in mist with seemingly never ending rains typical of the western slopes of the Cascade Mountains. When the sun does shine the canyon is spectacular with geologic formations such as Big Cliff at river mile 35 that make one feel lucky to live near the area.

Upper Clackamas River Log

Sandstone Bridge to Log Scaling Station

River mile: 48.5 to 35 .... 13.5 miles
Drift time: 2 hours 20 minutes .... 6 m.p.h.
Logged in kayak
River slope: 34 feet per mile average
River discharge: 2,300 c.f.s. Three Lynx gage
Recommended discharge: 1,000 to 5,000 c.f.s. Three Lynx gage
River discharge information:
    National Weather Service
    (503) 261-9246
Information:
    U.S. Forest Service
    Estacada District
    (503) 630-6861

UPPER CLACKAMAS RIVER

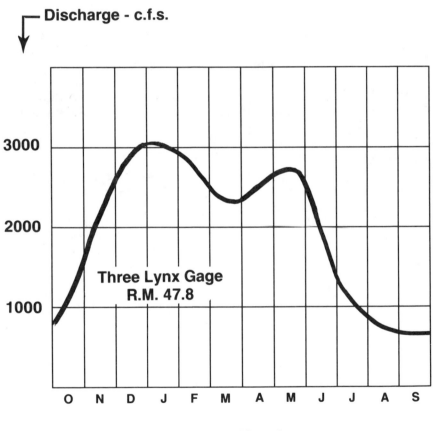

Discharge - c.f.s.

3000

2000

Three Lynx Gage
R.M. 47.8

1000

O N D J F M A M J J A S

Time - Months

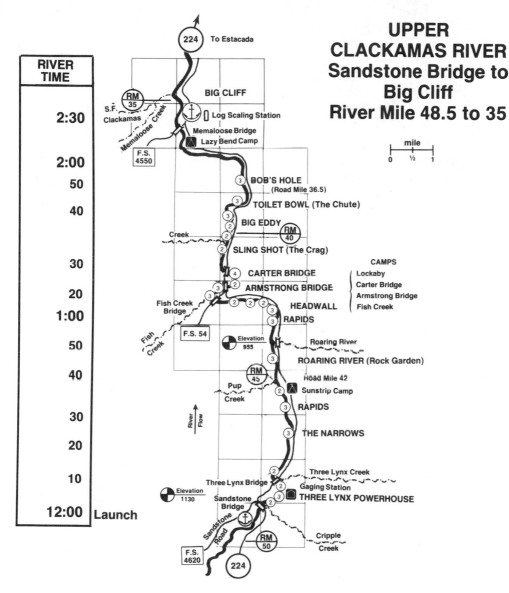

UPPER CLACKAMAS RIVER
Sandstone Bridge to Big Cliff
River Mile 48.5 to 35

Bob's Hole Competitor — Jeff Garren
First Place:
    Bob's Hole Rodeo, Oregon 1987, 1988, 1989, 1991
    Payette Rodeo, Idaho 1987
    Wenatchee Rodeo, Washington 1988
    LaPush Surf Pummel, Washington 1987

The Lower Clackamas River

Lower McIver Park to Mouth

The Lower Clackamas River is considered to be from the River Mill Dam above McIver Park at river mile 23.3 to its confluence with the Willamette River at West Linn. The section in this log is from an unimproved launch at the lower end of McIver Park to the mouth. This launch was selected to allow a relatively easy class two rapids difficulty trip involving about 17 rapids. There is a paved boat ramp at Upper McIver Park just below the Dam. Between the upper ramp and the lower launch are five rapids which border on class three difficulty at some river flows. Anyone with class three skills should not hesitate to start their trip at the upper boat ramp. The Lower Clackamas is a good place to develop whitewater skills before attempting more difficult whitewater.

The river has convenient access points allowing trips from 20 to 5 miles or less in length. Immediately after launching the boater comes into an area of river-front cottages, and the trip becomes more populated as one continues downstream, ending at Clackamette Park at the mouth.

In spite of being heavily used and close to urban areas, the Lower Clackamas River has a surprising amount of wildlife. The number of herons, osprey, kingfishers, turkey buzzards and common mergansers seem to increase each year. The fishing runs also appear to be improving, which means more power boats. Most of the power boats are fishermen who appear considerate in sharing the river with floaters. Portland area boaters can be thankful for a river like the Clackamas in their back yard. As the spring days lengthen, it's great to be able to put in a few hours paddling after work on this river.

Lower Clackamas River Log

Lower McIver Park to Mouth

River mile: 19.5 to 0 .... 19.5 miles
Drift time: 5 hours .... 4 m.p.h.
Logged in kayak
River slope: 13 feet per mile average
River discharge: 2800 c.f.s. Clackamas gage
Recommended discharge: 1500 to 5,000 c.f.s.
River discharge information:
    National Weather Service
    (503) 261-9246

LOWER CLACKAMAS RIVER

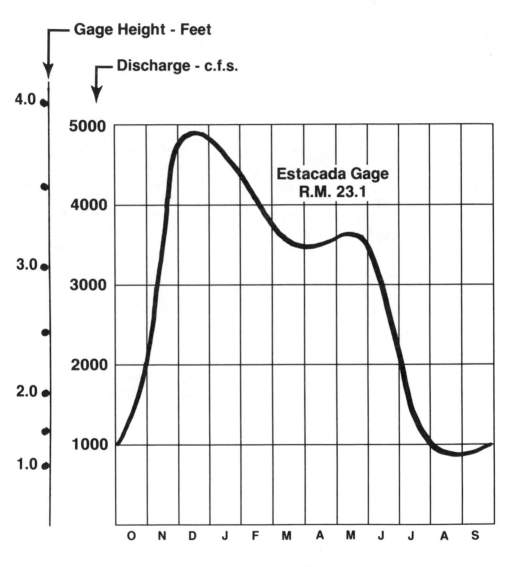

Gage Height - Feet

Discharge - c.f.s.

Estacada Gage
R.M. 23.1

Time - Months

28

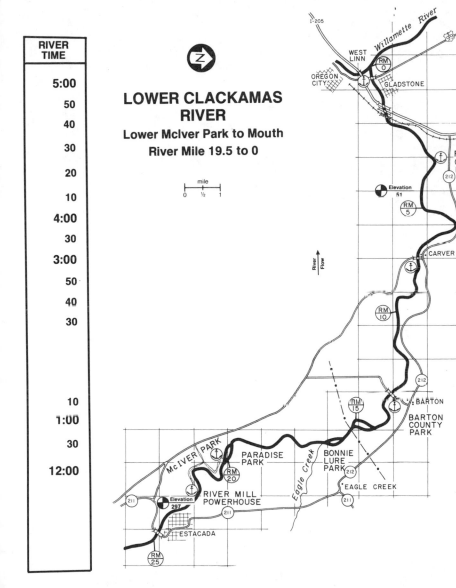

RIVER TIME	
5:00
50
40
30
20
10
4:00
30
3:00
50
40
30
10
1:00
30
12:00

LOWER CLACKAMAS RIVER

Lower McIver Park to Mouth
River Mile 19.5 to 0

mile
0   ½   1

River Flow

I-205

WEST LINN

Willamette River

OREGON CITY

GLADSTONE

RM 0

RIVERSIDE COUNTY PARK

212

Elevation 51

RM 5

CARVER

RM 10

212

RM 15

BARTON

BARTON COUNTY PARK

PARADISE PARK

BONNIE LURE PARK

McIVER PARK

Eagle Creek

212

EAGLE CREEK

RM 20

211

RIVER MILL POWERHOUSE

Elevation 297

211

211

ESTACADA

RM 25

29

Whitehorse Rapids — R.M. 76

Lower Whitehorse Rapids — R.M. 75

Upper Deschutes River

Highway 26 to Sherars Falls

The Deschutes River begins at Little Lava Lake south of Bend in central Oregon, near Wickiup Reservoir. From Wickiup Reservoir the river flows northerly entirely in Oregon to its confluence with the Columbia near The Dalles, a total length of 252 miles. The upper and lower sections referred to in this log include 97 miles from the state route 26 crossing of the river near Warm Springs to the mouth. The river has been divided by Sherars Falls; the upper section is from highway 26 to the falls and the lower section from Sherars Falls to the mouth. Together these log sections cover virtually the entire section included in the 1969 Oregon State Scenic Waterways System. The 1988 state rivers initiative and legislative action has given additional, more recent protection to other sections of the Deschutes. The Deschutes also received protection under the Federal Wild and Scenic River Act in 1988 as part of the Federal Omnibus Rivers Bill.

In this upper section of the Deschutes there are two different and distinct types of use. From the Rainbow launch (R.M. 97) to the locked gate (R.M. 59) there is limited public access. Public access is only at Trout Creek (R.M. 87) and at South Junction (R.M. 84), and South Junction does not have a boat ramp. Rafts and small craft are sometimes launched at South Junction by carrying craft across railroad tracks, then down a steep bank to the river. This upper section to the locked gate (R.M. 59) is a favorite section for fishing, and most trips are considered overnight camping trips of two or more days rather than day trips. Short day trips can be made from Rainbow launch to Trout Creek (R.M. 97-87).

Competition for camps in this area is critical. On some summer weekends more boaters launch than there are camps. This forces boaters to double camp, or they may just float downstream finally camping in desperation, possibly on private land. The Kaskela Flat, Davidson Flat areas near Whitehorse rapids are a logical first night camp. These are large areas in the scenic Mutton Mountains area and are often essentially full. Camping is complicated by boaters who send out lead boats, exchange camps or set up a vacant camp to be utilized later. Much of the left bank is private reservation land with no trespassing. Camps on the Deschutes are mostly in sagebrush country without many shade trees. Boaters should bring their own water and be aware that throughout most of the year open fires are prohibited.

From the locked gate (R.M. 59) to Sherars Falls (R.M. 44) there is frequent public access from a road paralleling the river on the right bank. This ready access makes the Maupin area the most used

31

whitewater boating section in Oregon. Most of the trips are from Harpham Flat (R.M. 56) to Sandy Beach (R.M. 45) before Sherars Falls. Boaters must exit at Sandy Beach and may not take out at Sherars Falls. On summer weekends the Maupin area lends itself to day trips, car camping and a semi-developed high use atmosphere. Kayakers who come to the Deschutes when other rivers are low congregate at "Surf City" just before Oak Springs rapids and "Elevator" just before Sand Beach. The continuous rafts along with more kayakers has caused them to coin a phrase from skiers. "The lift lines in Maupin are getting longer each year. "During mid-week the crowds are more reasonable.

For the whitewater boater there are three class 4 rapids in the upper section. Whitehorse rapids (R.M. 75), Train Hole (R.M. 54) and Oak Springs (R.M. 47) are the most difficult rapids in the upper section. Thousands of boaters run these rapids routinely along with class 3 rapids such as Buckskin Mary (R.M. 64), Wapinitia (R.M. 55), White River (R.M. 46) and Elevator (R.M. 45). The largest concentration of rapids is in the Maupin area which, along with easy access, accounts for the high use in this area. Sherars Falls has been run both on purpose and accidentally. Sherars is a class 6 falls. There are long stretches of flat water on the Deschutes interspersed with welcome rapids. The river moves along at a fast pace because of the relatively constant flow exceeding 4,000 c.f.s. throughout the summer. The Deschutes has reliable flows for boating the entire year.

Several raft rental liveries are available for boaters in the Maupin area. Car shuttles are available through the raft rental liveries both for boaters launching the upper Deschutes at Warm Springs or Trout Creek and also for the lower Deschutes. Shuttle service for the lower Deschutes is available also from The Dalles.

For the upper Deschutes trips, boaters often drive through Maupin and pick up a shuttle driver before unloading at the launch. Then the driver takes the car back to the Maupin take out. Vehicles should preferable not be left unattended, and should be parked in a supervised safe area during the trip until delivered at a specified time at the take out.

Upper Deschutes River Camps
Highway 26 to Sherars Falls

River Mile	Description	Left or Right Bank	Comments
45	Sand Beach	R	Boat Takeout - No Launch
46	White River	R	
47	Oak Springs, Upper	R	
47.5	Blue Hole	R	
48	Handicapped Ramp	R	
48.5	Gray Eagle Spring	R	
49	Spring Creek	R	
50	Oasis	R	
51	Maupin City Park	R	Boat Launch - Water
55	Wapinitia	R	Unimproved Boat Launch
55.5	Harpham Flat	R	Boat Launch
56.0	Long Bend	R	
56.5	Devils Canyon	R	
57	Nena Creek	R	
59	Locked Gate	R	
62.7	Buckskin Mary, Lower	R	
62.8	Buckskin Mary, Lower	R	
65	Dant	R	
65.6	Dant	L	
66	Dixon, Lower	R	
67	Dixon, Upper	R	
71.5	North Junction Bridge	R	Litter Station
72	Davidson Flat	R	Large Area
74	Railroad Tunnel	R	
75	Whitehorse, Lower	R	
75.3	Whitehorse, Lower	R	
77	Kaskela Flat	R	Large Area
80	Jersey School	R	
82	Axford	R	
84	South Junction	R	Difficult Launch Site

Elevator Rapids — R.M. 45

85	Redsides	R	
87	Gateway - Trout Creek	R	Unimproved Boat Launch
89	Island	R	
90	Basalt	R	
90.5	Frog Springs	R	
92	Mc-Island	R	
92.5	Crawdad	R	
93	Luelling	R	
94	Dry Creek	L	Access from ReservationCamp
94	Mecca Lower	R	
95	Mecca Upper	R	
97	Rainbow - Highway 26	R	Boat Launch

Surf City — R.M. 47

DESCHUTES RIVER

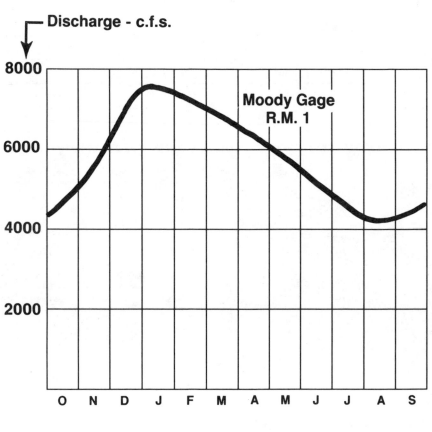

Discharge - c.f.s.

Moody Gage
R.M. 1

Time - Months

SHUTTLE MAP
DESCHUTES RIVER

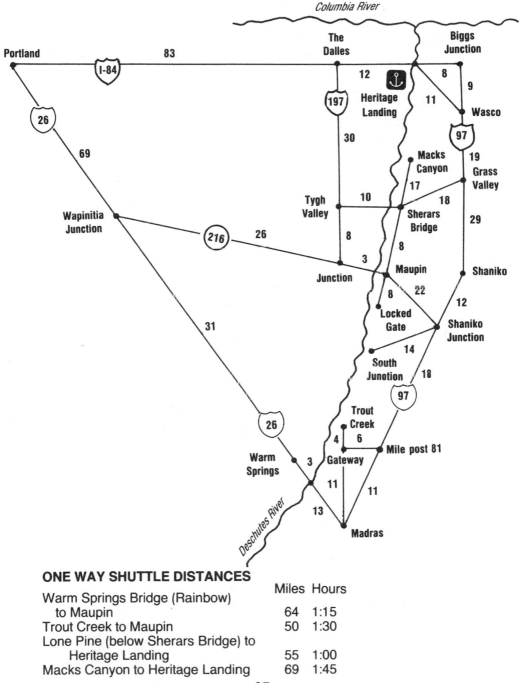

ONE WAY SHUTTLE DISTANCES

	Miles	Hours
Warm Springs Bridge (Rainbow) to Maupin	64	1:15
Trout Creek to Maupin	50	1:30
Lone Pine (below Sherars Bridge) to Heritage Landing	55	1:00
Macks Canyon to Heritage Landing	69	1:45

Upper Deschutes River Log

Highway 26 to Sherars Falls

River mile: 97 to 43 .... 54 miles
Drift time: 12 hours 25 minutes .... 4.3 m.p.h.
Logged in raft
River slope: 13 feet per mile average
River discharge: 4,500 c.f.s. Pelton Dam gage
Recommended discharge: 4,000 to 6,000 c.f.s. Moody gage
River discharge information:
    National Weather Service
    (503) 261-9246
Information:
    U.S. Bureau of Land Management
    Prineville District Office
    (541) 447-4115
    Day use passes required. Available at many sporting goods
    stores.

Limited access permits required on designated periods during summer.

Maupin car shuttles:
    The Oasis Resort (541) 395-2611
    River Runner Shuttle Service (541) 298-4004
    Most boat rental liveries arrange for shuttles.
Maupin boat rentals:
    River Trails (541) 395-2545 Maupin (503) 667-1964 Troutdale.
    Deschutes-U-Boat (541) 395-2503
    All Star Rafting 1-800-909-7237
    Deschutes Whitewater Services (541) 395-2232
    Ewings Whitewater 1-800-538-7238
    Deschutes River Adventures 1-800-723-8464
    C & J Lodge 1-800-395-3903
Maupin Lodging:
    C & J Lodge 1-800-395-3903
    The Oasis Resort (cabins) (541) 395-2611
    Deschutes Motel (541) 395-2626
    All Star Rafting (lodging) 1-800-909-7237

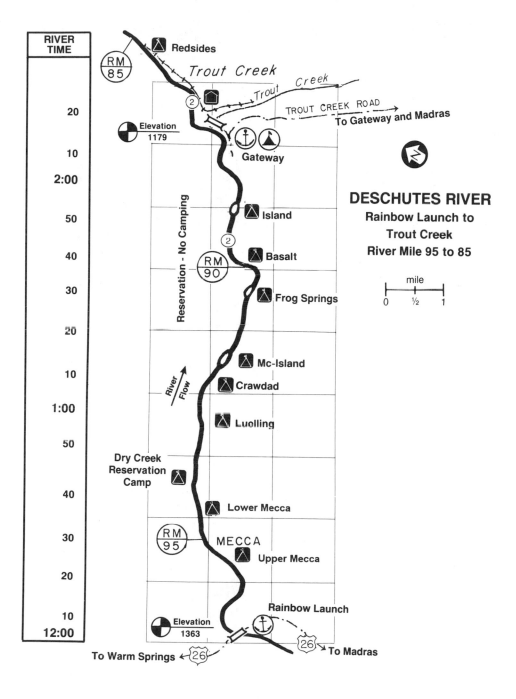

DESCHUTES RIVER
Rainbow Launch to
Trout Creek
River Mile 95 to 85

RIVER TIME

Redsides

Trout Creek

Trout Creek

TROUT CREEK ROAD

To Gateway and Madras

Elevation 1179

Gateway

Reservation - No Camping

Island

Basalt

Frog Springs

mile

0   ½   1

River Flow

Mc-Island

Crawdad

Luolling

Dry Creek Reservation Camp

Lower Mecca

MECCA

Upper Mecca

Rainbow Launch

Elevation 1363

To Madras

To Warm Springs ← 26

26 → To Madras

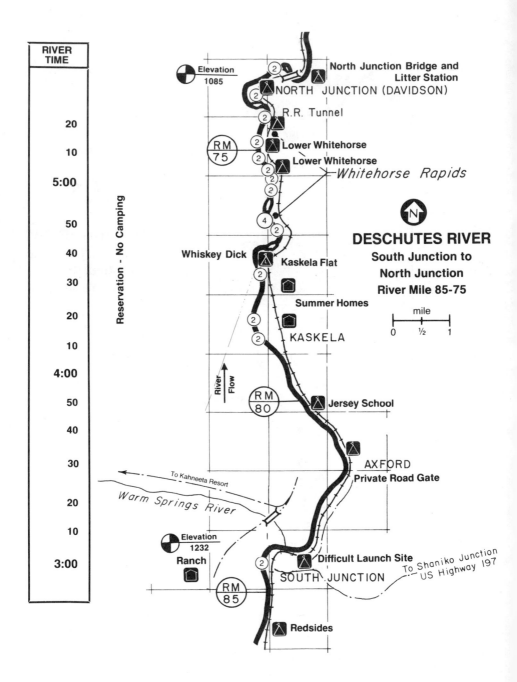

RIVER TIME

Reservation - No Camping

20
10
5:00
50
40
30
20
10
4:00
50
40
30
20
10
3:00

Elevation 1085

North Junction Bridge and Litter Station

NORTH JUNCTION (DAVIDSON)

R.R. Tunnel

RM 75

Lower Whitehorse

Lower Whitehorse

Whitehorse Rapids

N

DESCHUTES RIVER
South Junction to
North Junction
River Mile 85-75

mile
0   ½   1

Whiskey Dick

Kaskela Flat

Summer Homes

KASKELA

River Flow

RM 80

Jersey School

AXFORD

To Kahneeta Resort

Warm Springs River

Private Road Gate

Elevation 1232

Ranch

Difficult Launch Site

To Shaniko Junction
US Highway 197

SOUTH JUNCTION

RM 85

Redsides

40

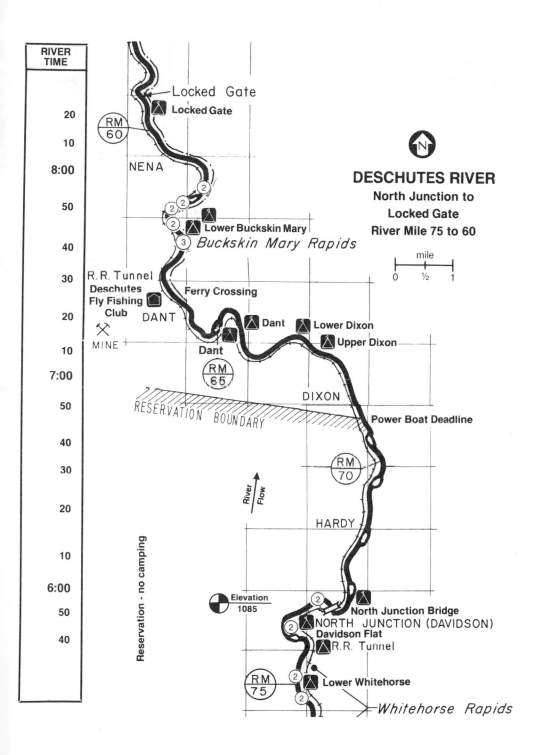

RIVER TIME

20
10
8:00
50
40
30
20
10
7:00
50
40
30
20
10
6:00
50
40

Locked Gate
Locked Gate

RM 60

NENA

②

②②
②
②
③ *Buckskin Mary Rapids*

Lower Buckskin Mary

R.R. Tunnel
Deschutes
Fly Fishing
Club
DANT

MINE

Dant

Ferry Crossing

Dant

Dant
Lower Dixon
Upper Dixon

RM 65

RESERVATION BOUNDARY

DIXON

Power Boat Deadline

RM 70

River Flow

HARDY

Reservation - no camping

Elevation 1085

②
North Junction Bridge
②
NORTH JUNCTION (DAVIDSON)
Davidson Flat
R.R. Tunnel

RM 75
②
②
Lower Whitehorse

Whitehorse Rapids

DESCHUTES RIVER
North Junction to
Locked Gate
River Mile 75 to 60

N

mile
0   ½   1

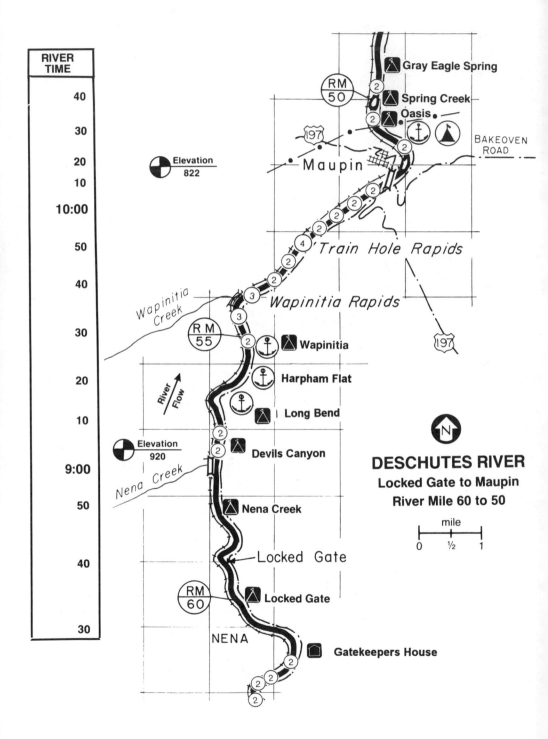

RIVER TIME

40
30
20
10
10:00
50
40
30
20
10
9:00
50
40
30

Gray Eagle Spring

RM 50

Spring Creek

Oasis

BAKEOVEN ROAD

197

Maupin

Elevation 822

Train Hole Rapids

Wapinitia Creek

Wapinitia Rapids

RM 55

Wapinitia

197

Harpham Flat

River Flow

Long Bend

N

DESCHUTES RIVER
Locked Gate to Maupin
River Mile 60 to 50

Elevation 920

Nena Creek

Devils Canyon

mile

0   ½   1

Nena Creek

Locked Gate

RM 60

Locked Gate

NENA

Gatekeepers House

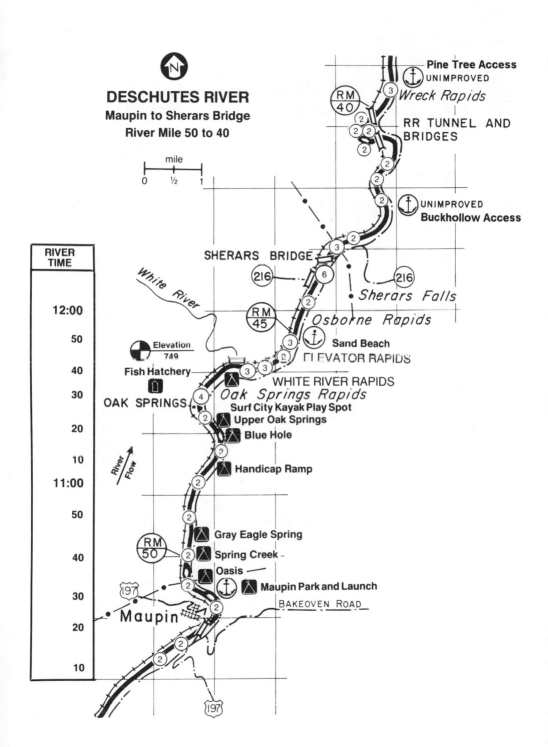

DESCHUTES RIVER
Maupin to Sherars Bridge
River Mile 50 to 40

mile
0   ½   1

Pine Tree Access
UNIMPROVED
Wreck Rapids
RR TUNNEL AND BRIDGES

UNIMPROVED
Buckhollow Access

RIVER TIME

12:00

50

40

30

20

10

11:00

50

40

30

20

10

SHERARS BRIDGE

216   216

Sherars Falls

RM 45

Osborne Rapids

White River

Sand Beach

ELEVATOR RAPIDS

Elevation 749
Fish Hatchery

WHITE RIVER RAPIDS

Oak Springs Rapids

OAK SPRINGS

Surf City Kayak Play Spot
Upper Oak Springs

Blue Hole

Handicap Ramp

River Flow

Gray Eagle Spring

RM 50

Spring Creek

Oasis

197

Maupin Park and Launch

BAKEOVEN ROAD

Maupin

197

43

Sherars Falls — R.M. 44

Sherars Falls — R.M. 44

Lower Deschutes River

Sherars Falls to the Mouth

Sherars Falls is the dividing line between the upper and lower Deschutes. The upper section was covered in the previous log. Sherars Falls is one of the few places where native Americans still hand net salmon as they have since the beginning of recorded time. There are petroglyphs at the falls which although still visible have unfortunatley been effaced by improper rubbing transfer techniques and vandals. There are cultural resources all along the Deschutes including important archaelogical sites which should receive the respect of recreationists.

The Lower Deschutes has two distinct types of recreation use governed primarily by access. From Sherars Falls to Macks Canyon (R.M. 25) the river is paralleled by the gravelled eighteen mile Bureau of Land Management access road. From Macks Canyon to the Columbia River there is no public vehicular access for boat launching. The access road section from the falls to Macks Canyon receives far less use than the nearby popular Maupin area. The gravelled access road section receives use from fishermen, campers, float boaters and some power boats. The major power boat use is from Macks Canyon to the mouth of the Deschutes.

A few boaters put in just below Sherars Falls at the Buckhollow access and run a short section to Pine Tree access at river mile 39, just below Wreck rapids. This section includes class 2 water to Wreck rapids which is a class 3. The Pine Tree access is a small unimproved place to launch. Many boaters start here as a convenience and to begin their trip in calm water. This gives beginning boaters a chance to develop some skills before encountering the major rapids near the take-out at the mouth. The access road section can be a day trip and also offers an opportunity for car camping or self-performing the shuttle.

During some times of the year there is very little use of the Lower Deschutes. When the steelhead are running it is quite a different matter. At that time float and power boaters congregate in great numbers, creating all the potential conflicts one might expect from high use, float/power conflicts and domination of camps by some boaters. There is a reluctance to enforce camp regulations, so some camps are in effect tied up almost exclusively by a few boaters. These quasi-permanent camps should not be confused with the three private camps above Lockit between river miles 15 and 14 on the left bank. When the steelhead count exceeds 2,000 per day at Bonneville Dam, fishermen flock to the lower Deschutes. Power boats take over, and the floater might just as well stay home. When it comes to competing for camps between floaters and power boaters it is no contest. As a result of the 1994 Deschutes River Management Plan, power boaters are now partially restricted on the upper and lower sections. See page 48 for motorized restrictions.

For boaters launching at Pine Tree, the river moves along at about four miles per hour, but there is no whitewater of any significance until reaching a new rapids called Washout, formed in 1995 at river mile 7. This rapids is under the transmission line crossing and upriver from Free Bridge near Kloan. Washout is a class four rapids and it is followed by four class three rapids called Gordon Ridge Rapids (R.M. 6), Colorado Rapids (R.M. 4), Rattlesnake Rapids (R.M. 3) and Moody Rapids (R.M. 1). In addition to these rapids, there are about 23 class 2 rapids to punctuate the long stretches that are rapid free. The lower Deschutes is famous for its upriver wind. It is no exaggeration when it is said winds may exceed forty miles per hour. Unanchored tents take the form of colorful tumbleweeds, and float boaters must bend to the oars during windy periods. The upriver wind usually comes up at noon as land warms and almost always occurs from Harris Canyon (R.M. 12) to the mouth.

Colorado Rapids — R.M. 4

Lower Deschutes River Camps*
Sherars Falls to Mouth

River Mile	Description	Left or Right Bank	Comments
1	Heritage Landing	L	Boat Ramp - Water
1	Deschutes State Park	R	Water
4	Colorado, Lower	R	
4.4	Colorado, Upper	L	
4.4	Colorado, Upper	R	
5.0	Camp	L	
5.2	Camp	R	
7	Kloan	L	
10	Fall Canyon	R	
11	Harris Canyon	R	
14	Lockit	L	
14-15	Three private camps - no trespassing	L	
18	Bull Run	R	
20	Camp	R	
21	Dike #2, Lower (Homestead)	R	
22	Dike #1, Upper	R	
25	Macks Canyon	R	Water, Boat Launch
30	Rattlesnake Canyon	R	
31	Beavertail	R	Water, Boat Launch
33	Gert Canyon	R	
34	Jones Canyon	R	
34.5	Oakbrook	R	
38	Twin Springs	R	
39	Lone Pine — Wreck Rapids Launch, No Camp	R	Unimproved Launch
42	Buckhollow, No Camp	R	Unimproved Launch

* Boaters use other informal camps, and new sites are under development.

Deschutes River Management Segments

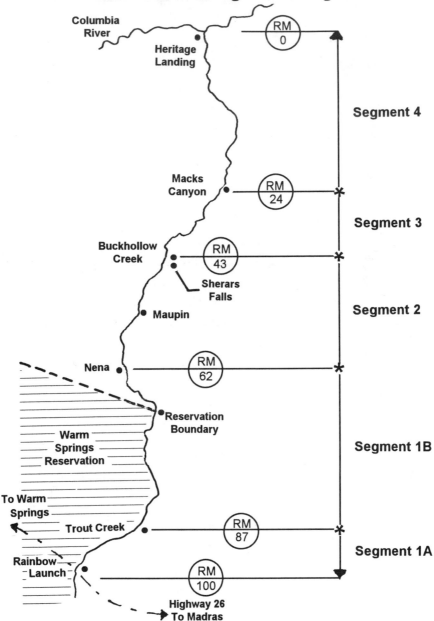

Motorboat Use Restrictions — 1996

Macks Canyon — Heritage Landing

> Motors prohibited alternating Thursday through Sunday periods begin-
> ning first weekend after June 15 continuing until September 30.

Buckhollow Creek — Macks Canyon

> Motors prohibited June 15 to September 30.

Warm Springs Reservation Boundary to Buckhollow Creek

> Motors prohibited May 15 - October 15.
>
> Motors allowed October 16 to May 14 with permit.

DESCHUTES RIVER

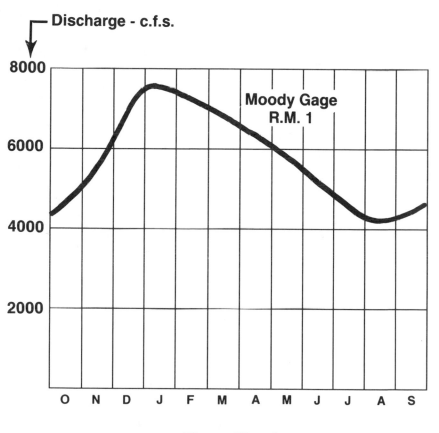

Discharge - c.f.s.

Moody Gage
R.M. 1

Time - Months

SHUTTLE MAP
DESCHUTES RIVER

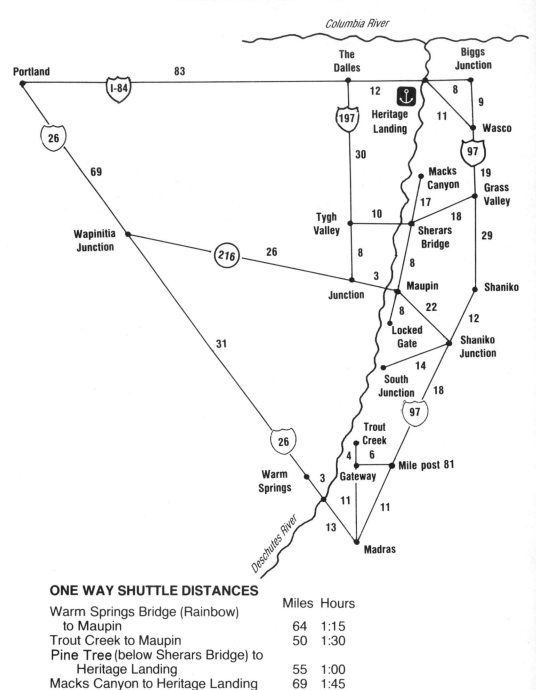

Columbia River

Portland

83 I-84

The Dalles

Biggs Junction

12 **8**

9

197 **Heritage Landing** ⚓

11

Wasco

97

26

69

30

Macks Canyon

19

Grass Valley

17

Wapinitia Junction

Tygh Valley **10**

18

216 **26**

Sherars Bridge

29

8

3

Junction

8

Maupin

Shaniko

8 **22**

12

31

Locked Gate

Shaniko Junction

14

South Junction **18**

97

26

Trout Creek

6

4

Mile post 81

Warm Springs **3** **Gateway**

11

11

13

Deschutes River

Madras

ONE WAY SHUTTLE DISTANCES

	Miles	Hours
Warm Springs Bridge (Rainbow) to Maupin	64	1:15
Trout Creek to Maupin	50	1:30
Pine Tree (below Sherars Bridge) to Heritage Landing	55	1:00
Macks Canyon to Heritage Landing	69	1:45

Lower Deschutes River Log

Wreck Rapids to the Mouth

River mile: 40 to 0 .... 40 miles

Drift time: 9 hours 35 minutes .... 4.2 m.p.h.
Logged in raft
River slope: 12 feet per mile average
River discharge: 5,400 c.f.s. Moody gage
Recommended discharge: 4,000 to 6,000 c.f.s.
River discharge information:
    National Weather Service
    (503) 261-9246
Information:
    U.S. Bureau of Land Management
    Prineville District Office
    (541) 447-4115
    Day use passes required. Available at many sporting goods
    stores.

Limited access permits required on designated days during summer.

Car shuttles:
    The Oasis Resort (541) 395-2611
    River Runner Shuttle Service (541) 298-4004
    Most boat rental liveries arrange for shuttles.
Maupin boat rentals:
    River Trails (541) 395-2545 Maupin (503) 667-1964 Troutdale.
    Deschutes-U-Boat (541) 395-2503
    All Star Rafting 1-800-909-7237
    Deschutes Whitewater Services (541) 395-2232
    Ewings Whitewater 1-800-538-7238
    Deschutes River Adventures 1-800-723-8464
    C & J Lodge 1-800-395-3903
Maupin Lodging:
    C & J Lodge 1-800-395-3903
    The Oasis Resort (cabins) (541) 395-2611
    Deschutes Motel (541) 395-2626
    All Star Rafting (lodging) 1-800-909-7237

RIVER MILE	RIVER TIME	LEFT BANK	RAPIDS	RIGHT BANK	DESCRIPTION
RM 20	4:00	▲ T			
	50				Dike Number Two
	40		2	▲ T	Dike Number One
	30		1 2		Three islands — Right past first, left past second and third.
	20		1		
	10		1	⚓ ▲ T	Macks Canyon (drinking water)
	3:00		1		
	50				
	40	~][~			Sinamox-Ferry Canyon
	30		1		
	20		1		
	10		1 1		
RM 30	2:00		1		Rattlesnake
	50		2	▲ T	Cedar Tree Island
	40		>2 1	▲ T	Beavertail (drinking water)
	30		2 1		
	20		2		Dumbell Drop Rapids
	10				
	1:00			▲ T	Girt Canyon
	50		2	▲ T	Jones Canyon
				▲ T	
	40		1 2	▲ T	Oakbrook
	30	~][~	1		
	20		2 1	▲	Twin Springs
	10		2		
	12:00		1 1	⚓	Lone Pine Launch
RM 40					

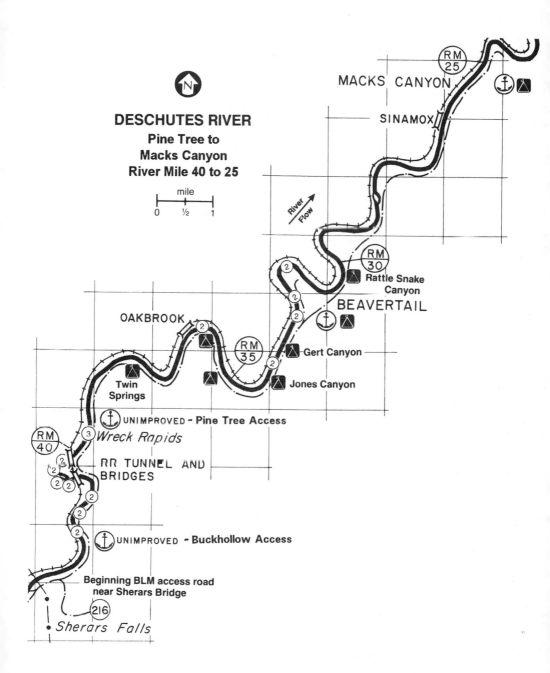

DESCHUTES RIVER
Pine Tree to
Macks Canyon
River Mile 40 to 25

mile
0   ½   1

River Flow

MACKS CANYON

RM 25

SINAMOX

RM 30

Rattle Snake Canyon

BEAVERTAIL

OAKBROOK

RM 35

Gert Canyon

Twin Springs

Jones Canyon

UNIMPROVED - Pine Tree Access

RM 40

Wreck Rapids

RR TUNNEL AND BRIDGES

UNIMPROVED - Buckhollow Access

Beginning BLM access road near Sherars Bridge

216

Sherars Falls

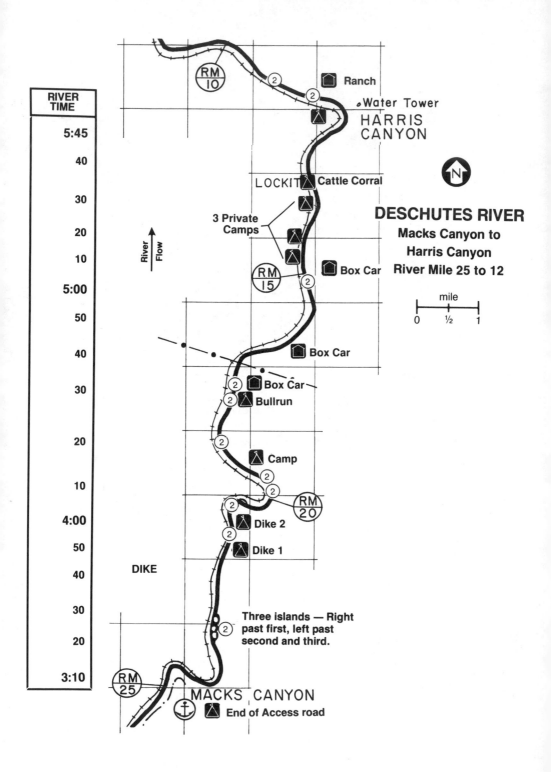

RIVER TIME	
5:45	
40	
30	
20	
10	
5:00	
50	
40	
30	
20	
10	
4:00	
50	
40	
30	
20	
3:10	

RM 10

2

Ranch

2

Water Tower

HARRIS CANYON

LOCKIT

Cattle Corral

3 Private Camps

RM 15

2

Box Car

Box Car

2

Box Car

2

Bullrun

2

Camp

2

2

RM 20

2

Dike 2

2

Dike 1

DIKE

Three islands — Right past first, left past second and third.

2

RM 25

MACKS CANYON

End of Access road

River Flow

DESCHUTES RIVER

**Macks Canyon to
Harris Canyon
River Mile 25 to 12**

mile

0   ½   1

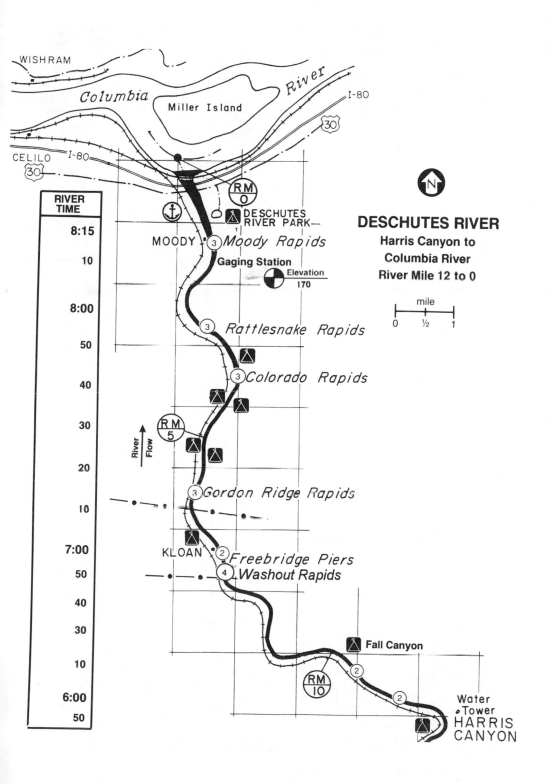

DESCHUTES RIVER

Harris Canyon to
Columbia River
River Mile 12 to 0

WISHRAM

Columbia *River*

Miller Island

I-80

CELILO

RIVER TIME

8:15
10
8:00
50
40
30
20
10
7:00
50
40
30
10
6:00
50

MOODY — *Moody Rapids*

DESCHUTES RIVER PARK

Gaging Station

Elevation 170

Rattlesnake Rapids

Colorado Rapids

RM 5

River Flow

Gordon Ridge Rapids

KLOAN — *Freebridge Piers*

Washout Rapids

Fall Canyon

RM 10

Water Tower

HARRIS CANYON

mile
0   ½   1

RM 0

55

Grande Ronde River — R.M. 60

Grande Ronde River

Minam to Troy

The Grande Ronde River originates in the Anthony Lakes area south of the town of LaGrande, then flows to the northeast corner of Oregon. The river flows through a short section of Washington where it joins the Snake River for a total river length of about 185 miles. The high mountain origins of the river hold snow for runoff until late in the year so boaters frequently use the river into July. Some of the tributaries of the Grande Ronde such as the Minam, are also used for boating, and part of the trip in this log is actually on the Wallowa river. The section described in this river log is from Minam to Troy, a distance of 46 miles. Boaters also drift the 45-mile section from Troy to the Grande Ronde's confluence with the Snake River. This latter 45-mile section is covered in the guide book Washington Whitewater 2, by Douglass A. North.

The Minam-Troy trip is in deep forested canyons that remind me of the Hells Canyon section of the Snake from Hells Canyon Dam to Johnsons Bar. The scale is smaller, but the similarity is there. The canyon is formed from visible layers of basalt that have weathered from natural erosion to form terraces. Between each vertical basalt ridge, slopes have formed where the grasses and predominant conifers grow. Horizontal shelves of trees with forest floor alternate with the rugged basalt cliffs. This area is famous for excellent deer and elk hunting. With rugged country, limited access and low population this is one of Oregon's most remote river trips.

You can expect to find a variety of wildlife on this trip. We saw geese, several species of ducks, deer, martin and all sorts of birds. We even had a bear and three rattlesnakes for company at the Bear Creek Camp. During our trip the hills were green, and purple lupine seemed to bloom everywhere. Later in the year the hills turn brown to match the bark of the pine, fir and tamarack trees that dominate the forest.

This is Chief Joseph country, and it is easy to see why the Nez Perce chose this area as their home. Throughout the Oregon river tours one cannot help being impressed with the fading signs of our past heritage. Only in remote areas do we see petroglyphs on the Snake and Owyhee Rivers, pit houses on the Snake or Deschutes Rivers, or the famous Nez Perce crossing on the Snake. One seldom sees these ancient signs on rivers near more populated areas. In the vast wilderness area in Oregon and Idaho that have remained largely unchanged, it is a tragedy the American people couldn't have found it in their hearts to let these native people live free and in peace on their own land.

The river trip starts either from Minam or from a state campground two miles downstream from Minam. The Minam River and Wallowa River merge at Minam, continuing as the Wallowa River for ten miles to Rondowa, where the river merges with the Grande Ronde. The usual river-mile convention is used in the log; river miles start from the mouth. This gives a unique mileage to any particular point on the river, so there is no mistaking when you say Sheep Creek Rapids is at river mile 79.3. You know the exact location.

River discharges for the Troy gage can be obtained daily from the National Weather Service. The Troy gage gives approximately 25 percent larger discharges than the Rondowa gage. The Troy gage is a good index of river condition and is used by most boaters because of convenience. At high discharges the river starts to approach flood stage, many of the sandy beaches are covered and the river is generally bank to bank. The Grande Ronde River has a steep river slope and you can expect high river velocity from the 21-feet-per-mile average river drop. Generally steep slopes are also associated with difficult boating for experts only, but the relatively constant river slope eliminates rapids the boater would expect to encounter in other pool and drop type rivers.

The river should prove enjoyable for boaters with intermediate or better boating skills. In this entire 46-mile trip there are only 4 major rapids. On our trip we ran all rapids without scouting, lining or portage. All types of boats run this river section: canoes, kayaks, McKenzie drift boats and rafts.

The main camps listed by the Forest Service are shown on the map. These sites are unimproved. Many other camps exist on the river and are shown in the log. Very few camps exist on the Wallowa River until near Rondowa. From Rondowa to Clear Creek on the Grande Ronde (R.M. 81-75) camps are also scarce. From Clear Creek to the trip end there are more campsites and some are large Ponderosa pine sites that are excellent. Camps are designated in the log simply as large or small, indicating a capacity of 30 or 10. Most of the trip is through grazing area, and some of the side streams are milky in appearance. Treating all river water used for drinking is recommended.

This section of the Grande Ronde can be boated in two days. However, we always try to stay longer because of the fine camps and scenery.

Most of the side streams on this trip are easily identifiable. This helps a great deal in locating Sheep Creek and Martins Misery rapids. The boater shouldn't have trouble orienting himself on this river.

Many boaters terminate their trip at the Powwatka Bridge, while others continue on to Troy or to the mouth of the Grande Ronde. Your terminus may depend partly on which route you intend to take on your return home. We have taken four different routes to get back to state highway route 82. The recommended main return route for those travelling south is to drive downriver from Troy to highway route 3. The roads through Flora, Powwatka or Palmer Junction are worthwhile alternate routes through some spectacular scenery with the possible opportunity to view deer, elk or an occasional bear. Although use of the Grande Ronde increases each year and is particularly heavy on holiday weekends, there are few areas or river trips in Oregon that can surpass the Grande Ronde as a wilderness experience.

Grande Ronde River Camps

River Mile	Name	Left or Right Bank	Camp Size Small, Medium, Large	Comments
(3.0)	Vincent (Powerline)	L	L	Wallowa River - Power Line Crossing
(2.5)	Miller Flat pasture	L	L	Wallowa River
(1.5)	Cabin Flat pasture	L	L	Wallowa River
79.3	Sheep Creek	R	L	
76.5	Unnamed	L	S	
76.5	Unnamed	R	S	
75.3	Clear Creek	R	S	Picnic Table Pit Toilet
75.1	Unnamed	L	L	
74.2	Unnamed	R	L	
73.8	Unnamed	L	S	
73	Unnamed	L	S	
73	Unnamed	R	S	
72	Unnamed	R	S	
71.8	Unnamed	R	L	
67	Martins Misery	L	S	
68	Unnamed	L	S	
68	Unnamed	R	L	
67	Unnamed	L	S	
66	Upper Bear Creek	L	L	Picnic Table Pit Toilet
66	Lower Bear Creek	L	S	Picnic Table Pit Toilet
65.5	Unnamed	R	L	
64.6	Unnamed	L	S	
64	Lower Elbow Creek	L	L	
63.5	Unnamed	L	L	
63.5	Unnamed	R	S	
62.5	Unnamed	L	L	Across from Grossman
62.5	Grossman Creek	R	S	

River Mile	Name	Left or Right Bank	Camp Size Small, Medium, Large	Comments
61	Island	R	L	
61	Island	L	L	
60.5	Promise Camp	R	L	
58.5	Upper Sickfoot	R	L	
58	Lower Sickfoot	L	L	
57.5	Eden Camp	R	L	
57	Island	R	L	
56.7	Unnamed	L	L	
56	Unnamed	R	L	
55.5	Unnamed	L	S	
54.8	Unnamed	L	S	
52.8	Powwatka Bridge Launch	R		No Camping
52.2	Mud Creek Launch	L		No camping Rocky Area
45.2	Troy Launch	R		No Camping At Bridge

Grande Ronde River Log

Minam to Troy

River mile: (10.0) to 45 . . . . 46 miles
  mileage in parenthesis is Wallowa River
Drift time: 9 hours 15 minutes . . . . 5.0 m.p.h.
Logged in raft
River slope: 21 feet per mile average
River discharge: 3100 c.f.s. Troy gage
Recommended discharge: 2,000 to 5,000 c.f.s. Troy gage.
River discharge information:
    National Weather Service
    (503) 261-9246
Information:
    Managed by U.S. Forest Service
    Walla Walla District
    (509) 522-6290
Car Shuttle:
    Minam Motel
    Minam, OR
    (541) 437-4475

61

GRANDE RONDE RIVER

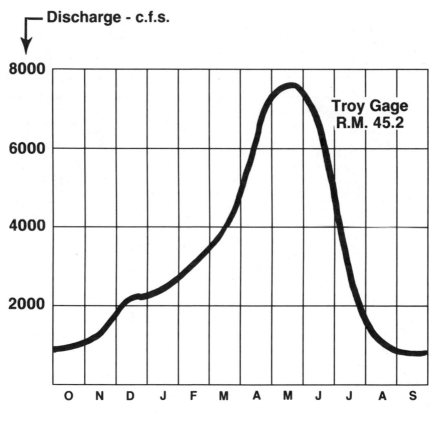

Discharge - c.f.s.

Troy Gage
R.M. 45.2

Time - Months

SHUTTLE MAP
GRANDE RONDE - SNAKE RIVERS

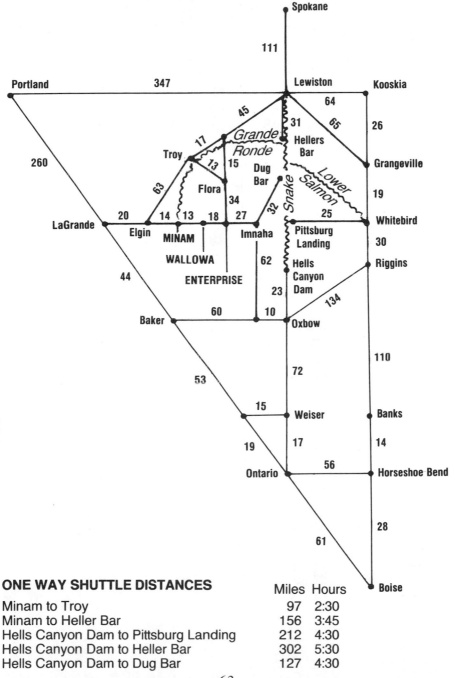

ONE WAY SHUTTLE DISTANCES

	Miles	Hours
Minam to Troy	97	2:30
Minam to Heller Bar	156	3:45
Hells Canyon Dam to Pittsburg Landing	212	4:30
Hells Canyon Dam to Heller Bar	302	5:30
Hells Canyon Dam to Dug Bar	127	4:30

63

RIVER MILE	RIVER TIME	LEFT BANK	RAPIDS	RIGHT BANK	DESCRIPTION
	4:00				
	50	～～～			Meadow Creek
	40	～～～			Creek
	30	⛺	⬭		
RM 75	20			⛺	
	10			⛺ T	Clear Creek (table, toilet)
	3:00			～～～	
	50				
	40				
	30				
	20		•2	🔺	SHEEP CREEK RAPIDS
	10	～～～			Sheep Creek Camp
81⁴ 0	2:00				
	50		⟞⟝	⬛	Rondowa Bridges - confluence
	40	🏠 ⛺		⛺	Cabin Flats camp area left
	30	⛺			Big Bench Camp area left
	20	⛺⛺⛺			Transmission Line camp area
	10		•2	⑤	Vincent Bridge right
RM 5	1:00	⑤	•2		LEDGE (BLIND FALLS) RAPIDS
	50	⑤			
	40				
	30		•2		HOUSE ROCK (RED ROCK) RAPIDS
	20	⛺	•2		State Campground
			2		MINAM ROLLER RAPIDS
	10				
RM 10	12:00	⚓			Minam Launch

64

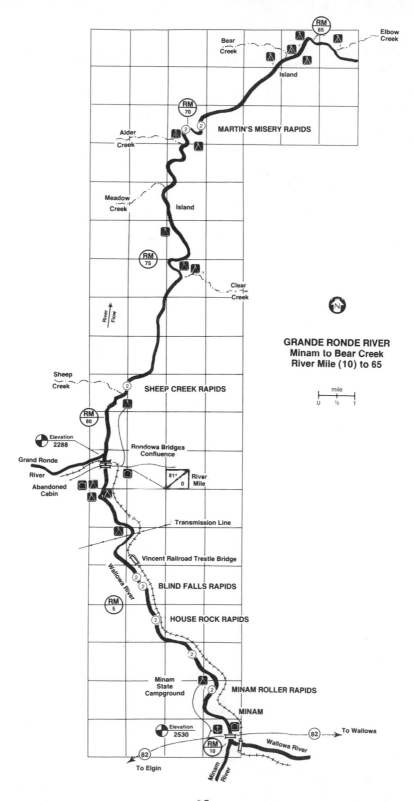

Bear
Creek

Elbow
Creek

RM 65

Island

RM 70

MARTIN'S MISERY RAPIDS

Alder
Creek

Meadow
Creek

Island

RM 75

Clear
Creek

River
Flow

GRANDE RONDE RIVER
Minam to Bear Creek
River Mile (10) to 65

mile

0   ½   1

Sheep
Creek

SHEEP CREEK RAPIDS

RM 80

Elevation
2288

Grand Ronde
River

Rondowa Bridges
Confluence

81+
0

River
Mile

Abandoned
Cabin

Transmission Line

Vincent Railroad Trestle Bridge

Wallowa River

BLIND FALLS RAPIDS

RM 5

HOUSE ROCK RAPIDS

Minam
State
Campground

MINAM ROLLER RAPIDS

MINAM

Elevation
2530

82

To Wallowa

RM 10

Wallowa River

82

To Elgin

Minam
River

RIVER MILE	RIVER TIME	LEFT BANK	RAPIDS	RIGHT BANK	DESCRIPTION
RM 45	9:15			⚓	Troy - out on right at bridge
	8:00				Ranch and farm area
RM 50	50	⚓		〰	Mud Creek Parking left
	40			⚓	Powwatka Bridge
	20			〰	Wildcat Creek
RM 55	10				
	7:00				
	50		⊙		Low Water Island
	40		⊙		Fourth Island
	30				Sickfoot Creek
	20		⊙		Third Island
RM 60	10		⊙		Second Island
	6:00				
	50		⊙		First Island
	40				Grossman Creek
	30			〰	
	20				Elbow Creek
RM 65	10				
	5:00				Bear Creek
	50				
	40		⊙		
RM 70	30		2 2		MARTINS MISERY RAPIDS UPPER MARTINS MISERY RAPIDS
	20	〰			Alder Creek — left
	10				
	4:00				

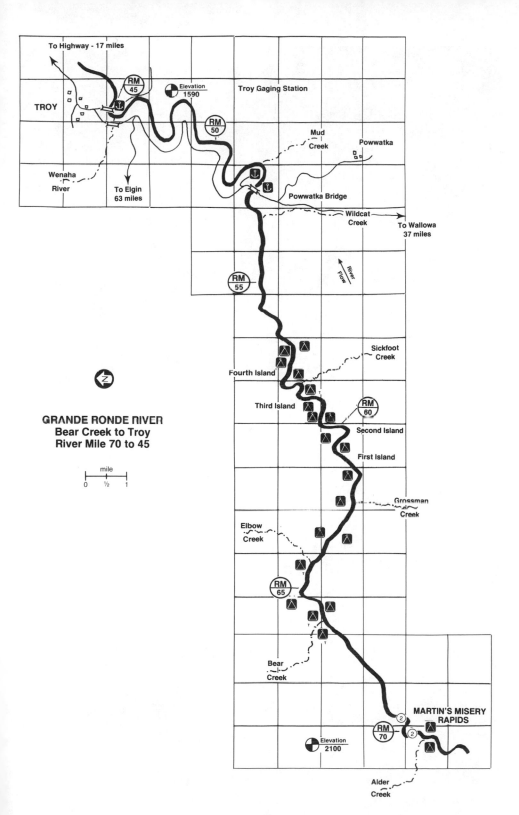

To Highway - 17 miles

RM 45

Elevation 1590

Troy Gaging Station

TROY

Mud Creek

Powwatka

Wenaha River

To Elgin 63 miles

RM 50

Powwatka Bridge

Wildcat Creek

To Wallowa 37 miles

River Flow

RM 55

N

Sickfoot Creek

Fourth Island

GRANDE RONDE RIVER
Bear Creek to Troy
River Mile 70 to 45

Third Island

RM 60

Second Island

First Island

mile
0   ½   1

Grossman Creek

Elbow Creek

RM 65

Bear Creek

MARTIN'S MISERY RAPIDS

2

RM 70

2

Elevation 2100

Alder Creek

Aquaduct Bridge Rapids — R.M. 11

Hood River

Hood River

Dee Bridge to Tucker Bridge

The Hood River drainage has its origins in glaciers on the northeast slopes of Mt. Hood. Small streams flow toward the Hood River valley merging as the East and West Forks of the Hood River near the town of Dee to form the main Hood River. A common launch for this trip is at the bridge just below the mill at Dee on the East Fork of the Hood. Another launch is at the confluence of the East and West Forks of the Hood River. Boaters also run a six mile section of the West Fork which includes portages at a fish ladder and at Punchbowl Falls. This log is for a seven and a half mile day trip beginning at the Dee Bridge and ending at the Tucker Bridge at river mile 6.1.

The first one and one half miles are on the East Fork of the Hood River. The river flows through a small wooded canyon with steep slopes and technical class three whitewater to the confluence with the West Fork of the Hood River at river mile 12.3, where the flow doubles and the canyon widens. The steep slope and rocky river channel make this technical class three run difficult to log because at flows about five feet on the gage (1450 c.f.s.) the river is continuous rapids. There are three rapids that stand out, however, as worth knowing about for at high flows they approach class four difficulty. The first is only a half mile from the East Fork launch at Dee Bridge. The second is at river mile 10.9 on a sharp right bend and is identified by a large silver truss aquaduct over the river. Don't confuse this bridge with the other two on the main Hood River, one a suspension bridge and one a bowstring shaped truss. The third major rapids is at an island at river mile 7.3. Take the right channel for a long rapids ending in a hole at the lower end of the island where the two forks of the river merge. There is a small island at river mile 8 just before the large island, and it serves as a warning for the island at river mile 7.3 and the rapids. Take the right channel at both of these islands.

This section of the main Hood River has a steep gradient of sixty four feet per mile and a rocky channel, making the run a continuous class two with at least six class three rapids in addition to those mentioned above. Boaters usually do not boat this section at gage heights of less than 4.0 — 4.5 feet.

The Hood River is most commonly boated during the months of March, April and May. An obviously popular river with the local boaters, it is also a favorite for Portland metropolitan area boaters. The section described can be boated in two hours, but the many play spots and the scenery on a sunny day suggest the more common trip time of three or more hours. In the spring when the apple blossoms are in bloom, the scenery adds much to the river run. Even the shuttle driver should enjoy this day trip, perhaps driving up the scenic Columbia River Gorge, then circling Mt. Hood through the Hood River Valley and stopping at Timberline Lodge for one of the most beautiful loop drives in Oregon.

Tucker Bridge

HOOD RIVER

Gage Height - Feet

Discharge - c.f.s.

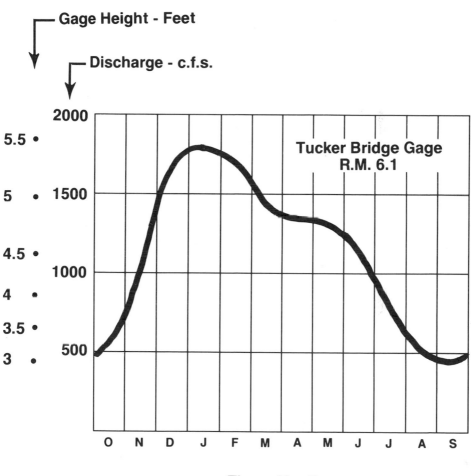

Tucker Bridge Gage
R.M. 6.1

Time - Months

Hood River Log

Dee Bridge to Tucker Bridge

River mile: (1.5) to 6.1 .... 7.7 miles
Drift time: 2 hours .... 4 m.p.h.
Logged in kayak
River slope: 64 feet per mile average
River discharge: 5.2 gage — 1600 c.f.s. Tucker Bridge gage
Recommended discharge: 4.5 to 6.5 Tucker Bridge gage
River discharge information:
    National Weather Service (503) 261-9246
*River mile in parenthesis are on East Fork Hood River. Trip includes
  1.5 miles East Fork and 6.2 miles on main Hood River.

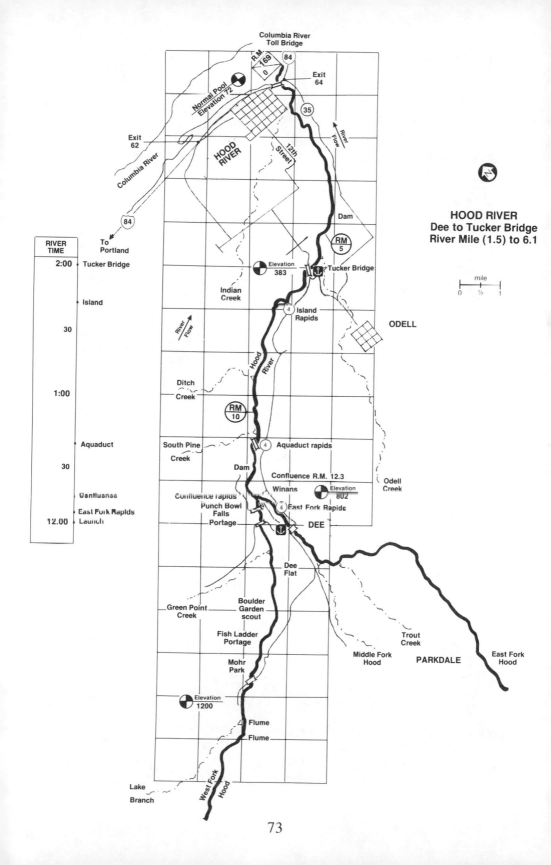

HOOD RIVER
Dee to Tucker Bridge
River Mile (1.5) to 6.1

Illinois River — R.M. 22

Illinois River

Miami Bar to Oak Flat

The headwaters of the Illinois River have their origins in California, but almost the entire 79 mile river length is in Oregon. Both the East and West forks of the Illinois begin in the rugged Siskiyou mountains at an elevation of 4,800 feet, then drop into a valley area near river mile 57, merging and continuing to the confluence with the Rogue River at Agness. Twenty-seven miles downstream from Agness the co-mingled waters of the Illinois and Rogue discharge into the Pacific Ocean. The Canyon section of the Illinois River is considered to be from its confluence to river mile 51, and the entire section of this 32 mile log is within the canyon area.

The Illinois River was a charter study river for inclusion in the National Wild and Scenic River System. Its sister river, the Rogue, was included in the original 1968 act as a National Wild and Scenic River. The Illinois is a major Rogue River drainage with more whitewater rapids and is more remote and wild than the Rogue. The Illinois is a wild and scenic whitewater river with clear blue-green water in a remote, heavily forested and rugged canyon. It achieved National Wild and Scenic River status in 1984.

The Illinois is a rain river, deriving its main water source from Pacific Ocean storms that quickly run off from the steep canyon drainage areas causing rapid rises and falls in the river. The snow that does accumulate in the higher elevations can combine with warm ocean rains to form devastating floods that scour the rocky canyons, causing frequent slide areas and, fortunately, flushing out most of the trees and log jams.

The canyon banks are lined with huge boulders, making landing for rafts sometimes difficult, and steep rock climbs of 20-40 feet in vertical elevation may be necessary in getting to the forest floor benches for campsites. Low water camps on occasional gravel bars are convenient but poor choices with a rising river and continuing rainstorms. Boaters are cautious about entering areas without camps, such as the four-mile section below the Green Wall, late in the evening with approaching darkness. All the camps are primitive, and some are little more than rocky niches lending themselves more to desperation than to comfort. One notable exception is Pine Flat (R.M. 27) with huge flat areas on both sides of the river just below Pine Flat Rapids. Access to Pine Flat camps also exists before the rapids. Once the boater recognizes that poison oak is a camping reality, it is possible to develop a positive attitude toward this primitive area. The

Pine Flat Rapids — R.M. 27

Prelude (Fawn Falls) Rapids — R.M. 19

Green Wall Rapids — R.M. 18

Green Wall Rapids — R.M. 18

Forest Service has designated the campsites shown on the campsite list.

As of 1996 there were no restrictions on the number of private boater permits. Self-issuing permits are required however, and they may be obtained at the Selma store. The maximum party size is 12 people.

After the boater passes Briggs Creek near the trip beginning there are no roads, and a trail parallels the river only part way. The few cabins that do exist and the river trail cannot be seen except by discerning boaters or those taking a hike away from the river. The steep canyon and the poison oak are not conducive to hiking by boaters.

Until recently there were very few boaters on the Illinois River. It was first logged by kayakers in 1973. In spite of the Illinois becoming an increasingly popular whitewater river, there are some deterrents to its use. It is a technically demanding river, the boating season is short and generally during cold spring months, requiring dry suits. Evacuation, particularly for an all kayak trip can be difficult. Nevertheless many people do have the necessary river skills and equipment and are willing to brave the sometimes chilling elements to experience this river.

The Kerby river gage at river mile 50 is the most generally used criteria for river flow data. Most boaters agree that desirable river flows are between 800 and 2,000 c.f.s. at the Kerby gage, and the optimum flow is about 1,200 c.f.s. Boaters who feel comfortable in big water consider 2,400 c.f.s. as being optimum, but most boaters will not boat this river above 3,000 c.f.s., and then only with a falling discharge and reasonable assurance from the weatherman that no severe rainstorms are in sight. Some significant sidestreams are added to the Illinois River within the canyon, and river volumes at the trip end may be three times greater than the Kerby gage flow.

The launch for this tour is 16 miles westerly from the town of Selma, Oregon, on the Illinois River road. Selma is 22 miles southwesterly from Grants Pass on route 199. The launch is unimproved with a road turnout and river gravel bar. This bar is called Miami Bar, or sometimes Oak Flat, and can accommodate several boats. The road extends a short way downstream to Briggs Creek, but launching upstream at Miami Bar allows a good warm-up rowing section before starting the major rapids below Briggs Creek.

The trip begins at an elevation of 825 feet at Briggs Creek and ends near elevation 97 at the confluence, for an average slope of 23 feet per mile. Although the 32 mile trip can be boated at highwater in a single day, most boaters prefer three or more days for the tour. The nine hours river log time is deceptive because, of course, it does not show the extra time taken to scout rapids or for other stops or delays.

The two most intense whitewater sections of the tour are from Panther Creek to just before Pine Flat (R.M. 31-28) and from Prelude Rapids (Fawn Falls) to Submarine Hole (R.M. 18-14). Rapids are of the pool and drop type with high frequency, averaging over three per mile, and, in some sections, one rapids seems to directly follow the other. Boaters should have class 4 skills in order not be intimidated by the river. There are numerous play spots for the kayaker. The class 4 rapids require technical maneuvering, with the potential of severe consequences for lack of skill. On our trip we scouted Pine Flat Rapids, the Green Wall and Submarine Hole. Pine Flat Rapids has a recommended sneak route on the left. The rapids is more difficult than first appears, and can easily flip a 16 foot raft. First-time boaters on the Illinois will want to scout the entire Green Wall section. You can run half of this long rapids and eddy behind a large boulder on the left. But if you miss this eddy, there is no alternative except to run the remaining class 5 rapids section. Kayakers can fairly easily carry around the lower half of the rapids from the eddy point, but portage for a raft is a herculean task. For this reason rafts are generally committed to running the Green Wall. This is the only class 5 rapids on the trip, although some boaters rate Pine Flats Rapids class 5, depending on their experience in running these rapids. Submarine Hole is worth a scout. Like most class 4 rapids it is straightforward when boated correctly, but has a dangerous keeper hole if you do it wrong.

A narrow section of the canyon ends at Submarine Hole, and by Collier Creek (R.M. 13) the canyon widens and takes on the characteristics of the Rogue River canyon. Rapids diminish in frequency and magnitude to the take-out at Oak Flat. There may originally have been some question about river designation for the Illinois in the minds of politicians, but there is no doubt to the whitewater boater. It is one of the best whitewater river tours in the West. On our last trip down the Illinois, I paused to look upstream just below Submarine Hole. A double rainbow framed the canyon as two colorful kayakers paddled downstream with the sun reflecting from glistening paddles that moved like perpetual motion windmills. The Illinois River is the end of the rainbow.

ILLINOIS RIVER

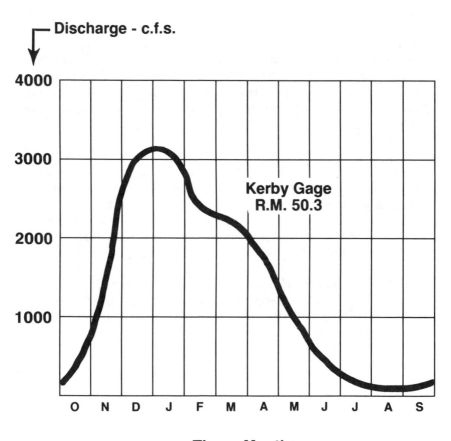

Discharge - c.f.s.

Kerby Gage
R.M. 50.3

Time - Months

Forest Service Designated
Illinois River Camps

River Mile	Name	Left or Right Bank	Camp Size Small, Medium, Large	Above High Water
32	Panther Bar	R	L	●
31	Nome Creek	L	S	●
29	Clear Creek	L	M	●
28	Upper Pine Flat	L	L	●
27	Lower Pine Flat	R	L	
27	Maidenhair Falls	L	L	●
26.5	Florence Creek	R	M	●
25	Klondike Creek	L	M	●
23	Deadman Bar	R	L	●
20	Unnamed Camp	R	S	
18	South Bend Mountain	R	M	
17	Unnamed Camp	L	S	
17	Green Wall	L	S	●
16.5	Unnamed Camp	R	S	●
13	Collier Creek	L	S	●
11	Miners Shaft	R	M	
10	Tri Falls	L	M	
10	Silver Creek	R	M	
6	Horsesign Creek	L	M	

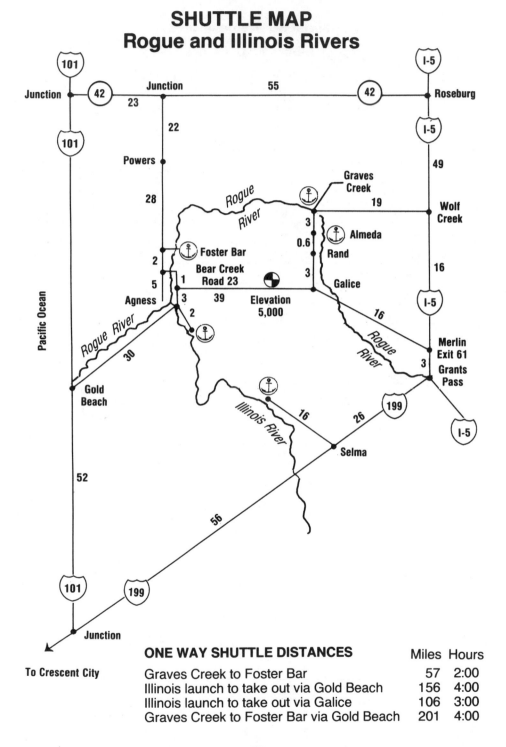

SHUTTLE MAP
Rogue and Illinois Rivers

101

Junction   42   Junction   55   42   Roseburg
              23

I-5

I-5

22

Powers   49

28   Rogue River   Graves Creek   Wolf Creek
                              19
                      3
                          Almeda
              0.6   Rand
      Foster Bar
2   Bear Creek   3   Galice   16
5   Road 23   1
Agness   3   39   Elevation   16
        2   5,000   Rogue River   I-5

Rogue River   Merlin Exit 61
                    3   Grants Pass
30
                    Illinois River
Gold Beach   16   26   199
                                    I-5
                    Selma

52

56

101   199

Junction

To Crescent City

ONE WAY SHUTTLE DISTANCES

	Miles	Hours
Graves Creek to Foster Bar	57	2:00
Illinois launch to take out via Gold Beach	156	4:00
Illinois launch to take out via Galice	106	3:00
Graves Creek to Foster Bar via Gold Beach	201	4:00

Illinois River Log

Miami Bar to Oak Flat

River mile: 35 to 3.5 .... 31.5 miles
Drift time: 9 hours 20 minutes .... 4 .m.p.h.
Logged in raft
River slope: 23 feet per mile average
River discharge: 1,000-1,300 c.f.s.
Recommended discharge: 800-2,500 c.f.s. (Kerby gage)
River discharge information:
    National Weather Service
    (503) 261-9246
Information: permits
    U.S. Forest Service
    Siskiyou National Forest
    Galice Ranger District
    P.O. Box 1131
    Grants Pass, OR 97526
    (541) 479-5301
    (541) 479-3755 (permits)
Shuttle:
    Galice Resort (541) 476-3818
Private boating permits are required from April 15 through June 30.
There are no limitations on number of permits issued (1996). Permits
are self-issuing at the Selma Store. Maximum party size is restricted
to 12 persons.

RIVER MILE	RIVER TIME	LEFT BANK	RAPIDS	RIGHT BANK	DESCRIPTION
	2:00				
	55	⛺		🏠	Shorty Noble Cabin
			4	〰	Clear Creek
	50				
			3		
	45				
	40			〉〉	Waterfall high on right
	35		4		
RM 30	30		2		
			4	〰	York Creek
	25				
	20				
	15		4		
	10		3		
	5		3		
	1:00	⛺	4		
	55		3		Labrador Creek
	50			〰	Panther Creek
				⛺	
	45				
	40		2	〰	Briggs Creek
	35		2		◑ Elevation 825° Briggs Creek
	30				
	25			🏠	Oak Flat Cabins
	20				
	15		2	〰	
	10		2	🏠	
	5	〰			
	12:00	〰		⚓	Launch
RM 35					

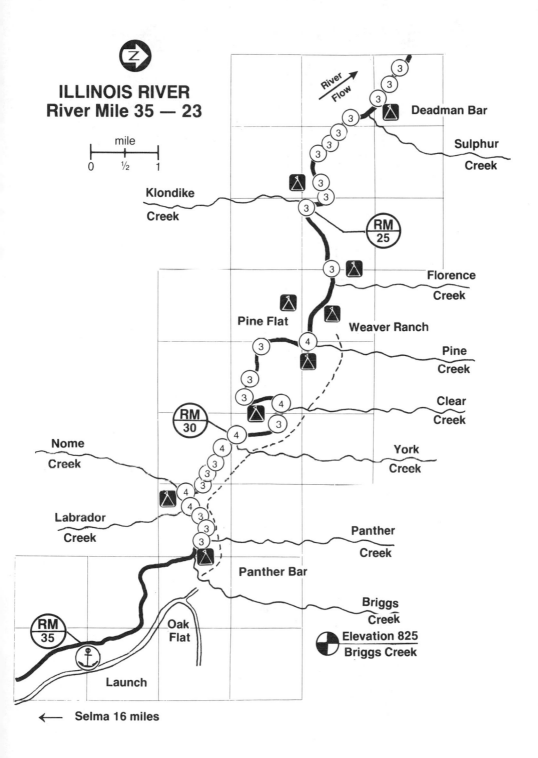

ILLINOIS RIVER
River Mile 35 — 23

mile

0   ½   1

River Flow

3
3
3
3   Deadman Bar
3
3
3   Sulphur
3   Creek
3
3
3   RM
3   25

3   Florence
                      Creek

Pine Flat   Weaver Ranch

3   Pine
4   Creek

3
3   4   Clear
RM   Creek
30   3
    4
Nome   4
Creek   3
            3
            4   York
Labrador   4   Creek
Creek   3
            3
                     Panther
                     Creek

                     Panther Bar
RM   Oak
35   Flat   Briggs
                                   Creek
⚓   Elevation 825
                                Briggs Creek
Launch

← Selma 16 miles

RIVER MILE	RIVER TIME	LEFT BANK	RAPIDS	RIGHT BANK	DESCRIPTION
•	4:00		• 3		
	55				
	50		• 3	~~~	
	45		• 3	~~~	
	40	~~~	• 3		
•	35	~~~	• 2	△	
	30	△		~~~	
	25		• 3		
RM 25	20	△	• 3	⌂	Klondike Creek
	15	~~~ △	• 3 • 2		
	10				
	5				
	3:00		• 3		
•	55			△	
	50	△	• 2	~~~	Florence Creek
	45	~~~	• 2 • 2	△	Pine Creek Rapids - scout
•	40				
	35	△	• 4	~~~	
	30		2	△	Pine Creek
	25	~~~	• 3		
RM 28	20			△	
	15	~~~	• 3		
	10		• 3	△	
	5		• 2	△	
	2:00		• 2		

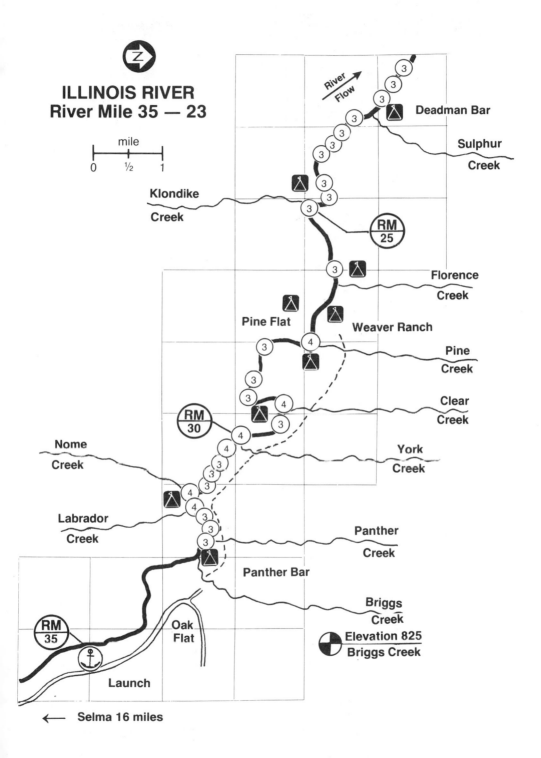

ILLINOIS RIVER
River Mile 35 — 23

mile

0   ½   1

River Flow

Deadman Bar

Sulphur Creek

Klondike Creek

RM 25

Florence Creek

Pine Flat

Weaver Ranch

Pine Creek

Clear Creek

Nome Creek

RM 30

York Creek

Labrador Creek

Panther Creek

Panther Bar

Briggs Creek

Elevation 825
Briggs Creek

RM 35

Oak Flat

Launch

← Selma 16 miles

RIVER MILE	RIVER TIME	LEFT BANK	RAPIDS	RIGHT BANK	DESCRIPTION
RM 15	6:00				
	55		4		
	50	~~~	3		
	45	~~~	2		
	40	~~~	3		
	35		2		
	30		4		
	25	⬛s	2 / 2	⬛s	Little Green Wall
	20		5		Green Wall Rapids - scout left
	15	⬛s	3	~~~	
	10	~~~	4		
	5				Prelude Rapids (Fawn Falls) Scout
	5:00	~~~	3		
	55		2		
	50				
RM 20	45	~~~		~~~	
	40	~~~	2 / 2	⬛s	Narrow Canyon
	35	~~~			
	30			~~~	
	25			~~~	
	20		2 / 2	~~~	
	15		2		
	10		3		
	5			⬛	Deadmans Bar
	4:00		2	~~~	
			3		

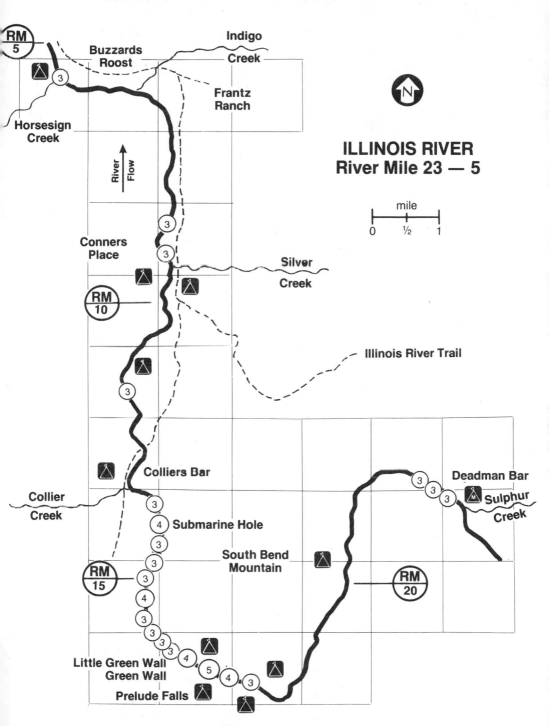

ILLINOIS RIVER
River Mile 23 — 5

GREEN WALL

RIVER MILE	RIVER TIME	LEFT BANK	RAPIDS	RIGHT BANK	DESCRIPTION
•	9:00				Confluence with Rogue at Agness
	55				
	50				Elevation 97° at Confluence
•	45				Take Out
	40			⚓	Lawson Creek
	35	~~~ 🏠			
	30			🔺	
	25		• 2		
RM 5	20	🔺			
	15	~~~	• 3		
	10		• 2		Horsesign Creek
•	5	~~~			Buzzards Roost — Proposed Dam
	8:00			~~~	Indigo Creek
	55		• 2	~~~	
•	50				
RM 8	45				
	40	~~~			
	35				
•	30	🔺	• 3	~~~	
	25		• 3		
	20	~~~			Waterfall left bank
	15	~~~ 🔺 🏠	• 2	~~~	Silver Creek
•	10		• 2	🔺 H.W.	
	5	🔺 H.W.			
	7:00			~~~	
•	55				
	50	~~~	• 3		
	45		• 2	🔺	
	40			~~~	
•	35		• 2		
	30	~~~	• 2		
	25	🔺 H.W.		~~~	
•	20	~~~	• 2		Collier Creek
	15		• 3		Narrow Canyon
RM 14	10		• 4		Submarine Hole Rapids - scout
	5		• 3		
	6:00	~~~	• 3		

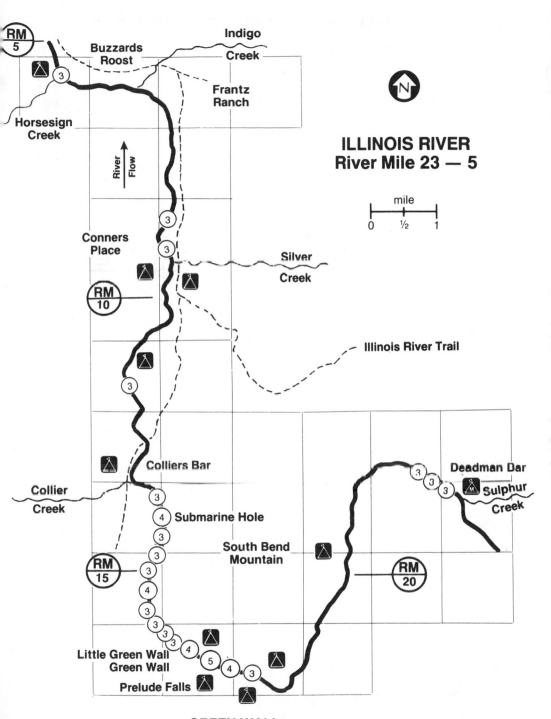

ILLINOIS RIVER
River Mile 23 — 5

RM 5

Indigo
Creek

Buzzards
Roost

Frantz
Ranch

3

Horsesign
Creek

River Flow

N

mile
0   ½   1

3

Conners
Place

3

Silver
Creek

RM 10

Illinois River Trail

3

3

Colliers Bar

Deadman Dar

3
3
3

Sulphur
Creek

Collier
Creek

3

4   Submarine Hole

3

South Bend
Mountain

RM 20

RM 15

3

3

4

3

3
3
3   4

5   4   3

Little Green Wall
Green Wall

Prelude Falls

GREEN WALL

Prelude (Fawn Falls) — R.M. 18   Jim Jordan

Submarine Hole — R.M. 14

To Powers

To Galice

mile
0   ½   1

Shasta Costa
Creek

Agness

Rogue River

27
0   RM

Confluence
Elevation   97°

Gold Beach
27 miles

Illinois River

Oak Flat

River
Flow

Nancy
Creek

Lawson
Creek

Indigo
Creek

RM
5

Buzzards
Roost

3

Frantz
Ranch

Horsesign
Creek

9

93

Burnt Ranch Rapids — R.M. 132

Upper John Day River

Service Creek to Clarno

The John Day River originates about thirty miles east of the town of John Day and, as Oregon's longest river, flows 275 miles northwesterly to its confluence with the Columbia River. The section from Service Creek at river mile 157 to Tumwater Falls at mile 10 is a State Scenic Waterway and also has federal protection under the National Wild and Scenic Rivers Act. By popular usage the section from Service Creek to Clarno is referred to as the Upper John Day and from Clarno to Cottonwood bridge is the Lower John Day. This log is for the Upper John Day.

In the section from Service Creek to Clarno the John Day River provides a water route through eastern Oregon cattle ranching country, and some outstanding scenery in Oregon's Blue Mountain geological province. The entire trip is in cattle grazing area coupled with some sections, such as the Twickenham or Clarno areas, that are irrigated farm land. The John Day River is unregulated except for large irrigation withdrawals, so the river fluctuates between wide limits. During the 1964 flood the Service Creek gage recorded 40,200 c.f.s.

In normal years the river becomes low around the first of June, and in summer it is an unboatable trickle of water. April and May are the most popular boating periods.

The Upper John Day is a relatively easy boating section with only three class two-three rapids depending on river flow. The recommended discharges for boating are 1,500-4,000 c.f.s.; however, boaters do float at much higher river discharges. This section of the river is an enjoyable overnight tour, usually lasting three or more days. Some boaters use the Service Creek to Twickenham section as a convenient day trip.

There is no formal camp list for this trip. However, there are adequate primitive areas for camping. The camps in the log were selected simply by judgement as places with relatively easy boat landing and in large areas with trees for protection from the elements. An effort was made to avoid selecting camps in irrigated farm areas or on posted land. Boaters should carry their own water, or treat river water, as evidence of cattle grazing is everywhere. Campers should plan on burying or, preferably, carrying out human waste. Foregoing open fires in this rangeland, except in case of emergency, is good river ethics.

The most scenic area of the Upper John Day tour is from Burnt Ranch to Eagle Canyon, approximately river mile 132-118. There

95

Russo Rapids — R.M. 150

Upper John Day — R.M. 123

are side canyons for hiking, and, during the spring, geese and ducks are nesting along with a large variety of other birds. At proper river levels the small mouth bass fishing can be "hot". With luck boaters can sometimes see eagles soaring on the thermals along the canyon rims. In spring the John Day can vary from warm sunny days to freezing nights, and afternoon winds can be fierce. In good weather this is not an area to hurry through. Plan an extra layover day to just relax in camp or hike. Stop a few moments at Rajneeshpuram to see the desolate failed enterprise returning to the dozen cattle caretakers and the sagebrush.

Clarno Bridge — R.M. 109

Upper John Day River

JOHN DAY RIVER

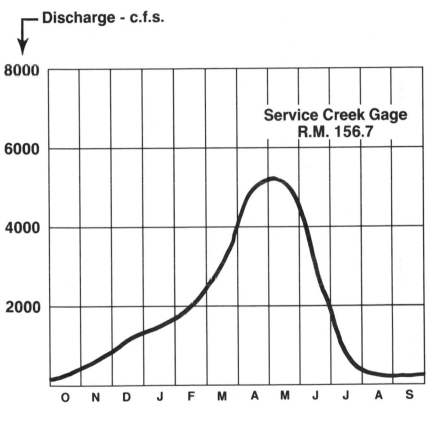

Discharge - c.f.s.

8000

6000

4000

2000

Service Creek Gage
R.M. 156.7

O N D J F M A M J J A S

Time - Months

SHUTTLE MAP
JOHN DAY AND
NORTH JOHN DAY RIVERS

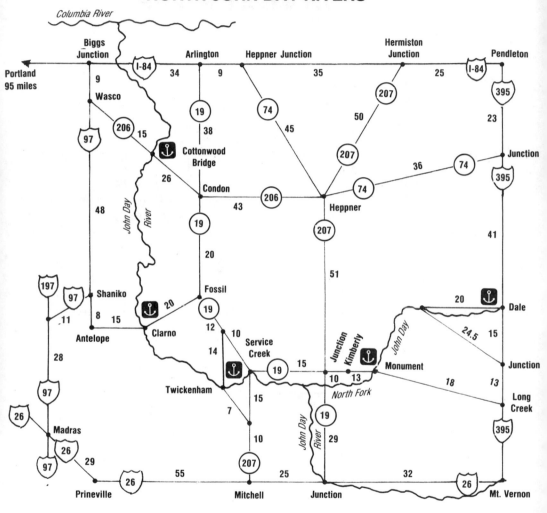

ONE WAY SHUTTLE DISTANCES	Miles	Hours
Dale to Monument	46	1:00
Service Creek to Clarno	42	1:00
Clarno to Cottonwood	66	1:15

100

Upper John Day River Log

Service Creek to Clarno

River mile: 158 to 109 .... 49 miles
Drift time: 13 hours 40 minutes .... 3.6 m.p.h.
Logged in raft
River slope: 8 feet per mile average
River discharge: 2,400 c.f.s. Service Creek gage
Recommended discharge: 1,500 to 4,000 c.f.s.
River discharge information:
    National Weather Service
    (503) 261-9246
Information:
    U.S. Bureau of Land Management
    Prineville District Office
    P. O. Box 550
    Prineville, OR 97743
    (541) 447-4115
Car shuttle:

    Service Creek Trading Post
    (541) 468-3331

    The Shamrock
    Box 302
    Fossil, OR 97830
    (541) 763-4896

RIVER MILE	RIVER TIME	LEFT BANK	RAPIDS	RIGHT BANK	DESCRIPTION
	4:00				
	50		·—··—··		Overhead powerline
	40				
	30		⊏⊐		Twickenham Bridge
RM 145	20		·—··—··		Twickenham Valley Ranch area.
	10	🏠 🏠	(·)		
	3:00				
	50				
	40	⛺ ⛺	· 1	🏠	Sheep ranch
	30				
	20	⛺	· 1		
RM 150	10		1	🏠	
	2:00				
	50		· 2	⛺	RUSSO RAPIDS
	40				
	30				
	20	⛺ ⛺			
	10		(·)		
	1:00			⛺ ⛺	
	50	⛺ ⛺	(·)		
RM 155	40	🏠	· 1		Abandoned farm
	30		(·)		
	20	⛺			
	10	◑	1 · (·) 1	🏠	Ranch Gage station, left
	12:00		⊏⊐	⚓	Launch

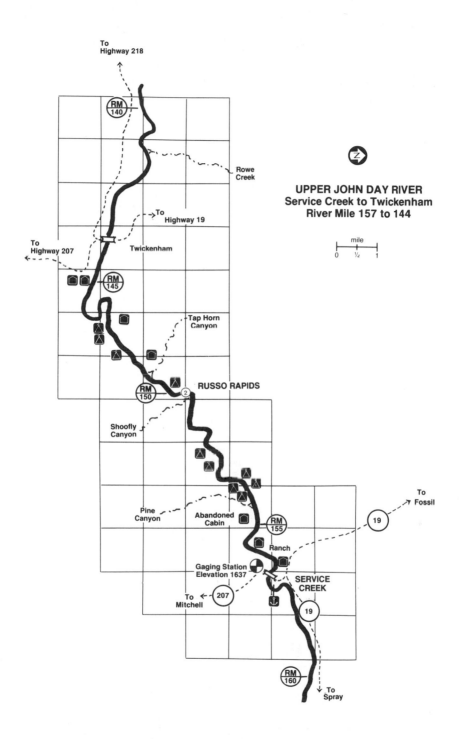

UPPER JOHN DAY RIVER
Service Creek to Twickenham
River Mile 157 to 144

To
Highway 218

RM
140

Rowe
Creek

To
Highway 19

To
Highway 207

Twickenham

RM
145

Tap Horn
Canyon

RUSSO RAPIDS

2

RM
150

Shoofly
Canyon

To
Fossil

Pine
Canyon

Abandoned
Cabin

RM
155

19

Ranch

Gaging Station
Elevation 1637

SERVICE
CREEK

To
Mitchell

207

19

RM
160

To
Spray

mile
0   ½   1

RIVER MILE	RIVER TIME	LEFT BANK	RAPIDS	RIGHT BANK	DESCRIPTION
RM 130	8:00				
	50				
	40				
	30				
	20	⛺	• 1		camp above river near road
	10	⛺	• 2	🛶	BURNT RANCH RAPIDS
	7:00		• 1		
	50		• 1		
	40	🏠			
RM 135	30	🏠			Large 20' high rock mid-channel
	20				
	10		1		
	6:00	🛶			
	50				
	40				
	30			🛶	
	20	🏠	• 1	⛺	Abandoned building, left
	10	⛺	⊙	⛺ 🛶	
	5:00	⛺ 🛶	• 2		FOSSIL RAPIDS
	50		• 1		
RM 140	40				
	30				End Twickenham Valley area
	20				
	10		·—·—··		Overhead power line
	4:00				

104

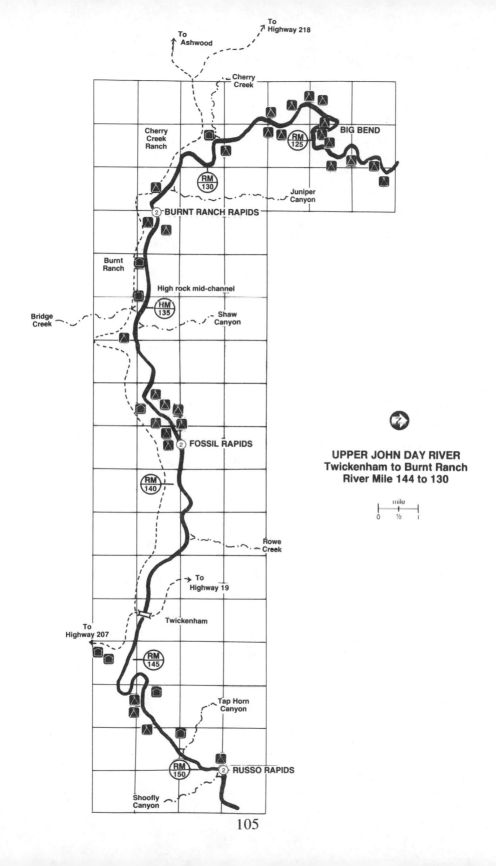

To
Ashwood

To
Highway 218

Cherry
Creek

Cherry
Creek
Ranch

BIG BEND

RM
125

RM
130

2 BURNT RANCH RAPIDS

Juniper
Canyon

Burnt
Ranch

High rock mid-channel

HM
135

Shaw
Canyon

Bridge
Creek

FOSSIL RAPIDS

RM
140

Rowe
Creek

To
Highway 19

To
Highway 207

Twickenham

RM
145

Tap Horn
Canyon

RUSSO RAPIDS

RM
150

2

Shoofly
Canyon

UPPER JOHN DAY RIVER
Twickenham to Burnt Ranch
River Mile 144 to 130

mile
0   ½   1

RIVER MILE	RIVER TIME	LEFT BANK	RAPIDS		RIGHT BANK	DESCRIPTION
	14:00					
	50					
	40		[bridge]		[anchor]	Clarno Bridge Launch
RM 110	30	[house]				Abandoned schoolhouse
	20		–·–·–			
	10		–·–·–			
	13:00			[⊙]		
	50		–·–·–		[house]	
	40		–·–·–			Overhead powerlines
RM 115	30		–·–·–			
	20					
	10					
	12:00	[house]				
	50	≈≈≈	–·–·–			Rajneeshpuram left
	40					High Fence, overhead powerlines. Muddy Creek left.
	30					
RM 120	20					Road along right bank Possible kayak take out
	10					Large columnar basalt cliff, left
	11:00	[camp]			[camp]	
	50				[camp] [camp]	Beginning of farm area continues to Clarno launch.
	40					
	30		[⊙]	1		
	20			1	[camp] [camp]	
	10				[camp]	Whistling Bird Camp Upper Whistling Bird Camp
	10:00		1 [⊙]		[camp]	
RM 125	50		[⊙]			Island camp - access lower end of island
	40	[camp]				
	30	[camp]		1		"S" Turn Camp
	20		[⊙]		[camp]	Big Bend Camp
	10	[camp] [camp]			[camp]	
	9:00	[camp]				
	50				[camp]	
	40	[camp]			[camp]	
	30					
	20		–·–·–			
RM 130	10	[house]		1 [⊙]	[camp]	
	8:00					

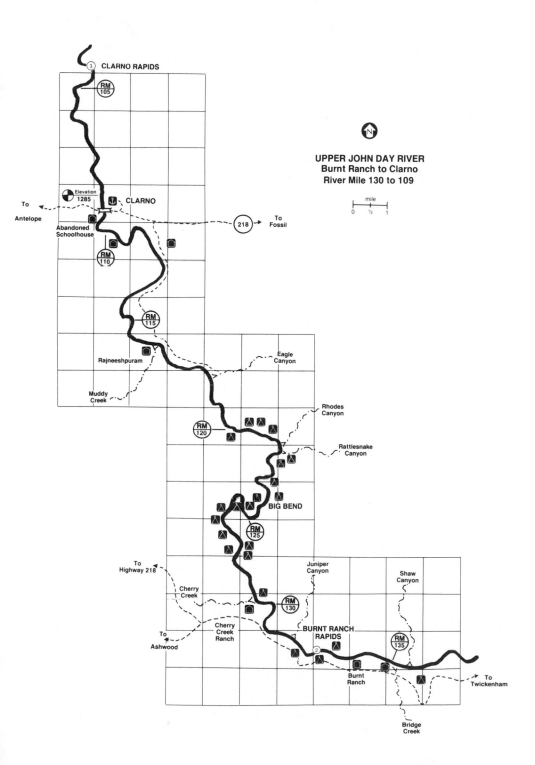

CLARNO RAPIDS

RM
105

Elevation
1285

CLARNO

To
Antelope

Abandoned
Schoolhouse

RM
110

To
Fossil

218

RM
115

Rajneeshpuram

Eagle
Canyon

Muddy
Creek

Rhodes
Canyon

RM
120

Rattlesnake
Canyon

BIG BEND

RM
125

To
Highway 218

Cherry
Creek

Juniper
Canyon

Shaw
Canyon

RM
130

BURNT RANCH
RAPIDS

RM
135

To
Ashwood

Cherry
Creek
Ranch

Burnt
Ranch

To
Twickenham

Bridge
Creek

UPPER JOHN DAY RIVER
Burnt Ranch to Clarno
River Mile 130 to 109

mile

0   ½   1

Red Wall Camp — R.M. 92

Lower John Day River

Clarno to Cottonwood Canyon Bridge

The John Day River is Oregon's longest river, originating in the Blue Mountains thirty miles east of the town of John Day and flowing over 275 miles to the Columbia River. The section from Service Creek at river mile 157 to Tumwater Falls at river mile 10 was a designated State Scenic Waterway in the 1969 initiative petition legislation and has since received federal protection under the National Wild and Scenic Rivers Act. The river has been divided by popular usage at Clarno (R.M. 109), and Service Creek to Clarno is referred to as the Upper John Day and Clarno to Cottonwood Canyon Bridge where highway 206 crosses the river is called the Lower John Day. Tumwater Falls makes it impractical to boat below the Cottonwood Bridge. This log is for the Lower John Day trip.

The John Day River is relatively unregulated; however, there are large irrigation withdrawals that influence how long each year it is practical to boat the river. During the December 1964 flood the flow at Service Creek was 40,200 c.f.s. During the summer the river can be an unboatable trickle of water. River flow is governed primarily by the high elevation of the river's source, so it is a snow runoff river that peaks in May and is unrunnable by late July.

Being an undammed river the John Day has a high silt load, making it a "brown" river at high runoff. The John Day begins at high elevation in the forested Blue Mountains, but the Lower John Day section is in a semi-arid unforested area typical of the Columbia Basin uplands. The river has carved a major canyon two thousand feet deep in some areas, and this Great Basalt Canyon is the main attraction of the trip.

The Lower John Day trip begins at the Clarno bridge boat launch, and for the first ten miles the boater is in relatively flat water coursing through irrigated farm and ranch land. The only major rapids is Clarno at river mile 105. There is a farm road on the left bank which boaters can drive along to scout Clarno Rapids before beginning this sixty-nine mile trip. The eleven feet per mile average river slope means that the velocity will be approximately 3-4 miles per hour at flows of 2,000-5,000 c.f.s.

Other than Clarno Rapids, there are about a half dozen class two rapids and two dozen class one rapids. Obviously, boaters find merit in the John Day other than its rapids. Although this is grazing land with cultivated, fenced land and ranches along the way, there is a feeling of solitude and remoteness as this river has relatively low use except during the Memorial Day weekend.

Lower John Day River — R.M. 77

Wagon Camp — R.M. 75

The dramatic basalt canyon walls begin near Basalt Rapids (R.M. 95) and continue intermittently throughout most of the trip. In some areas huge diced basalt monoliths have tumbled from canyon rims down talus slopes and, occasionally, into the river to complicate boating. The basalt is scoured black at the water line, and oxidizes to reds further up the canyon walls. The deep, wide canyon seems to fuse into solid tan and red colors.

The recommended flow for the Lower John Day trip is 2000-5000 c.f.s. Some boaters run the river at high water of 10,000 c.f.s. or higher. At high water Clarno rapids becomes a long series of large chocolate-colored waves rather than the sharp drop followed by rock dodging that occurs at lower flows. While high water does increase river velocity and hydraulics, the river still can be a reasonable trip for boaters with intermediate skills who feel comfortable in big water. During flood stage the side canyons introduce river gravels which are deposited as channel islands by the main river. As flows decrease, these islands become exposed making more than one river channel from which the boater must choose. The island outruns result in the several minor rapids boaters encounter on the trip.

Camps on this tour are often on the benches of the inside curve of the meandering river. Usually there are cobbles and gravel at the water line, and the benches are ten or more feet above the rocky shore line. The river benches support mostly sagebrush and juniper trees with easily-ignited cheat grass. Boaters should guard against range fires by cooking near the river and by having a bucket of water nearby. Open fires are a poor choice on the John Day. There are lots of areas in which to camp along the river, but many are open, windy and show the ever-present signs of cattle. Some areas, particularly near the end of the trip, have few camps. All the camps are primitive, indicating that the carry-out or burial method of human waste disposal is required.

Although the Lower John Day is considered a relatively easy whitewater river, there are other considerations for the boater wishing to make this an enjoyable tour. At normal flows a raft trip will take 16 to 20 hours of river time, and boaters sometimes do not allot sufficient time for the trip. Attempting the Lower John Day on a three-day weekend with the good possibility of strong upriver afternoon winds and perhaps doing your own shuttle, may mean getting home very late or missing a day at work. Boaters should bring plenty of water in case they have underestimated their time on the river. In an emergency boaters may be able to find a green "seep" in the side gullies, but they shouldn't count on it. This area may also experience extremes in temperature, and often warm clothing will be more practical than a swim suit. Good trip planning is the best insurance for an enjoyable tour. Boaters who do their home work will find floating the Great Basalt Canyon and the Lower John Day a rewarding experience.

JOHN DAY RIVER

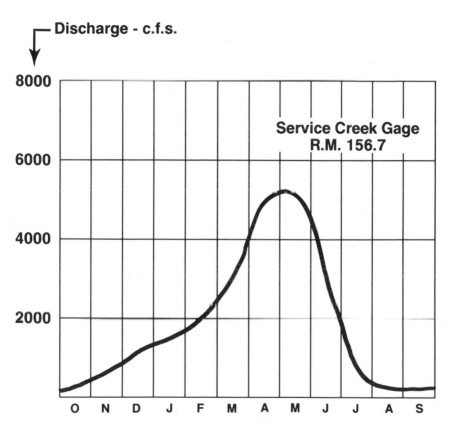

Discharge - c.f.s.

Service Creek Gage
R.M. 156.7

8000

6000

4000

2000

O N D J F M A M J J A S

Time - Months

SHUTTLE MAP
JOHN DAY AND
NORTH JOHN DAY RIVERS

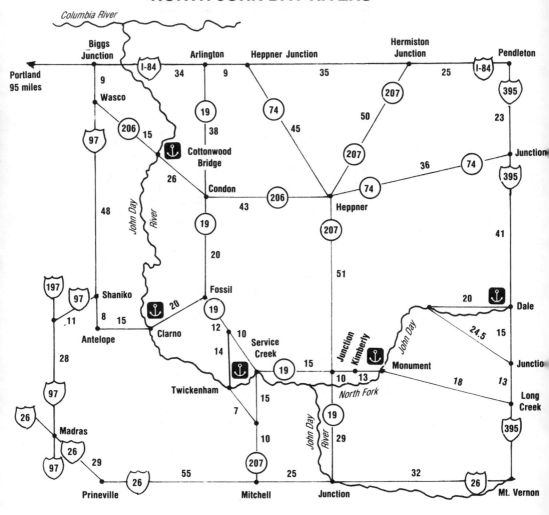

ONE WAY SHUTTLE DISTANCES	Miles	Hours
Dale to Monument	46	1:00
Service Creek to Clarno	42	1:00
Clarno to Cottonwood	66	1:15

114

Lower John Day River Log

Clarno to Cottonwood Canyon Bridge

River mile: 109 to 40 .... 69 miles
Drift time: 16 hours 15 minutes .... 4.3 m.p.h.
Logged in raft
River slope: 11 feet per mile average
River discharge; 2800-3200 c.f.s. Service Creek gage
Recommended discharge; 2,000-5,000 c.f.s.
River discharge information:
    National Weather Service
    (503) 261-9246
Information:
    Managed by U.S. Bureau of Land Management
    Prineville District
    P. O. Box 550
    Prineville, OR 97754
    (541) 447-4115
Shuttle information:
    Jim and Jeanette Wallace
    Rufus, OR 97050
    Service Station at Rufus — I-84 Exit 109
    (541) 442-5750 — Home
    (541) 739-2887 — Work (Service Station)

    The Shamrock
    Box 302
    Fossil, OR 97830
    (541) 763-4896

RIVER MILE	RIVER TIME	LEFT BANK	RAPIDS	RIGHT BANK	DESCRIPTION
	4:00		2		
	50				BASALT RAPIDS
RM 97	40		⊙ 1		Large basalt boulders in channel
	30				Island Camp
	20				Ranch - power lines
	10		1		
	3:00		2		Barn
	50				Basalt rocks in channel
	40				Power lines
	30				
RM 105	20				
	10		1		Power lines - Island
	2:00		⊙ 1		Power lines - Island
	50		1		Power lines
	40		⟩ 1		
	30		2 ⟨ 3		Mulberry Spring Camp
	20		⟩ 2		CLARNO RAPIDS, scout left
	10		2		
	1:00				
	50		1		
	40				
	30				
	20			farm land	
	10				
RM 109	12:00			⚓	Launch - Clarno Bridge

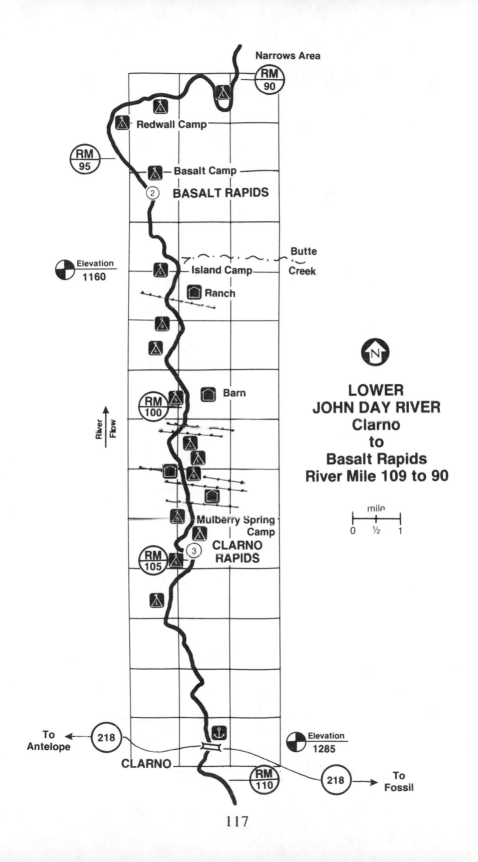

Narrows Area

RM 90

Redwall Camp

RM 95

Basalt Camp

② BASALT RAPIDS

Elevation 1160

Island Camp

Butte Creek

Ranch

River Flow

Barn

RM 100

LOWER
JOHN DAY RIVER
Clarno
to
Basalt Rapids
River Mile 109 to 90

mile
0   ½   1

Mulberry Spring
Camp

③ CLARNO
RAPIDS

RM 105

To
Antelope

218

Elevation 1285

CLARNO

RM 110

218

To
Fossil

117

RIVER MILE	RIVER TIME	LEFT BANK	RAPIDS	RIGHT BANK	DESCRIPTION
RM 75	8:00			⛺	
	50	⛺		⛺	Old wagons, right
	40			⛺	
	30	⛺			Horseshoe Bend
				⛺ 🏠	Columnar Basalt Wall Camp
	20		1		Small shack
	10			⛺	
		⛺			
RM 80	7:00	⛺	1		
	50	⛺	1		
	40	⛺ ⛺			
	30				
	20				
	10		1	🏠	Ranch right
RM 85	6:00	〰〰〰	1		Pine Hollow Creek, left
	50	⛺			
	40				
	30				Four boulders in channel
					Canyon, right
	20				
RM 90	10				Narrows area
	5:00	⛺			
	50				
	40		1		Island
	30			⛺ ⛺	Redwall Camp
	20		1		Columnar Basalt Wall, right
RM 95	10		2		
	4:00		>1	⛺	Basalt Rapids Camp

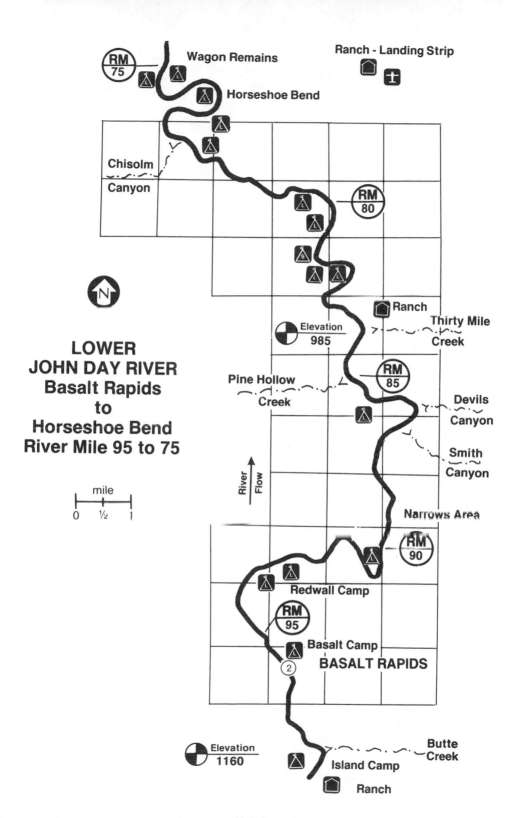

RM 75

Wagon Remains

Ranch - Landing Strip

Horseshoe Bend

Chisolm Canyon

RM 80

Ranch

Elevation 985

Thirty Mile Creek

LOWER JOHN DAY RIVER Basalt Rapids to Horseshoe Bend River Mile 95 to 75

Pine Hollow Creek

RM 85

Devils Canyon

Smith Canyon

River Flow

mile

0   ½   1

Narrows Area

RM 90

Redwall Camp

RM 95

Basalt Camp

2

BASALT RAPIDS

Elevation 1160

Island Camp

Butte Creek

Ranch

119

RIVER MILE	RIVER TIME	LEFT BANK	RAPIDS	RIGHT BANK	DESCRIPTION
	12:00				
	50			⛺	Lower Hoot Owl Camp
	40		1		
RM 60	30	⛺			Hoot Owl rock right
	20		1	⛺ ⛺	
	10	∿∿∿		⛺	Jacknife Creek Canyon
	11:00			⛺	
	50		1		
	40		1		
	30				
RM 65	20				Red, white, blue graffitti right
	10				Island
	10:00			⛺	
	50	⛺ ⛺			Island
	40		1		
	30			⛺	
	20				
RM 70	10		1 ⊙		Island
	9:00				
	50				
	40		1		
	30				
	20		1	⛺	Island
	10				
	8:00				
RM 75					

120

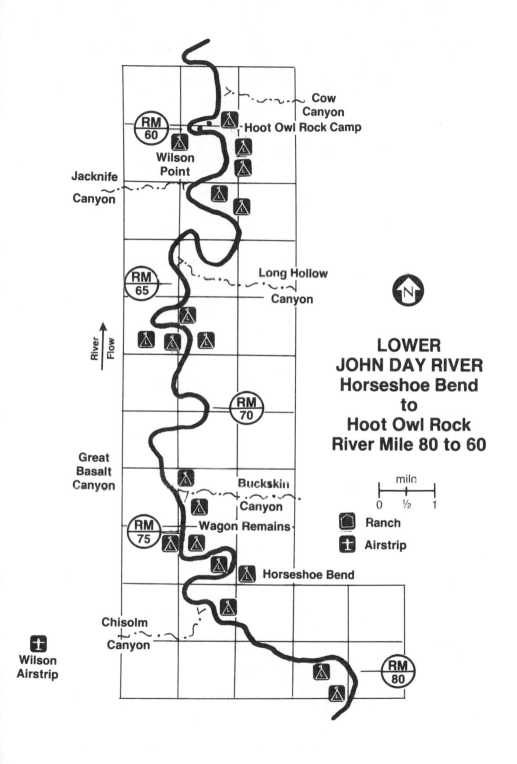

Cow Canyon

Hoot Owl Rock Camp

RM 60

Wilson Point

Jacknife Canyon

RM 65

Long Hollow Canyon

River Flow

N

RM 70

LOWER
JOHN DAY RIVER
Horseshoe Bend
to
Hoot Owl Rock
River Mile 80 to 60

Great Basalt Canyon

Buckskin Canyon

Wagon Remains

RM 75

Horseshoe Bend

Chisolm Canyon

Wilson Airstrip

RM 80

mile

0   ½   1

⬡ Ranch

✝ Airstrip

RIVER MILE	RIVER TIME	LEFT BANK	RAPIDS	RIGHT BANK	DESCRIPTION
	10			⚓	Take out - Cottonwood Bridge
RM 40	16:00				
	50	～＜			Canyon
	40				
	30			△	Transmission towers horizon
	20				
	10				
	15:00				
RM 45	50	△			Two pole power line horizon / Islands
	40	～＜			Willow Spring Canyon left
					Transmission Towers high on left
	30			△	
	20	⌂ △		＞～	Abandoned cabin left / Canyon right
	10				Two pole power line on horizon
	14:00				
	50		⊙		Island
RM 50	40		1		
	30		⊙		Island
	20	△	1		
	10				Island
	13:00		1 ⊙	＞～	Ferry Canyon
	50				
	40		1		Island
	30	～	1 ⊙		Little Ferry Canyon
RM 55	20				
	10			△	
	12:00			＞～	Cow Canyon

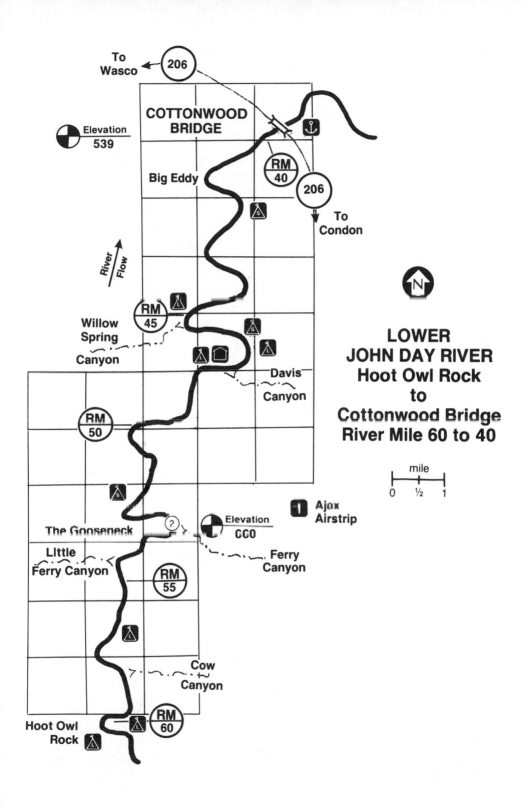

To
Wasco

206

COTTONWOOD
BRIDGE

Elevation
539

Big Eddy

RM
40

206

To
Condon

River
Flow

RM
45

Willow
Spring

Canyon

Davis

Canyon

RM
50

N

LOWER
JOHN DAY RIVER
Hoot Owl Rock
to
Cottonwood Bridge
River Mile 60 to 40

mile

0   ½   1

The Gooseneck

2

Elevation
CCO

Ajax
Airstrip

Little
Ferry Canyon

Ferry
Canyon

RM
55

Cow
Canyon

RM
60

Hoot Owl
Rock

Great Basalt Canyon

Lower John Day River — R.M. 60

Horseshoe Bend — R.M. 77

North Fork John Day

North Fork John Day River

Camas Creek to Monument

The North Fork of the John Day is a 112 mile tributary of the main John Day River. The river begins in the Blue Mountains just south of Anthony Lake and east of the North Fork John Day Wilderness Area. The high elevation of its origins make this a snow melt controlled river whose peak runoff usually occurs in May. The section described in this tour begins near the community of Dale at the Camas Creek Bridge at river mile 56.5 and continues downstream 40 miles to the town of Monument.

The average stream slope of 18 feet per mile and the relatively smooth channel make this a relatively fast river. At moderate flows this should be a reasonable tour for intermediate boaters. There are perhaps 20 class two rapids, which above 2,000 c.f.s. tend to wash out and below 2,000 c.f.s. begin to present rock problems. Most boaters will want to boat at discharges above 2,000 c.f.s. at the Monument gage.

The North Fork of the John Day River flows are not a regular part of the National Weather Service recording. A good estimate of the Monument gage flows, however, is 70 percent of the John Day River flows at the Service Creek gage, which is a part of the recording.

This river tour begins at the confluence of Camas Creek with the North Fork of the John Day, or downstream on the right bank at any convenient launch, as there are no formal launch sites. The river flows westerly for about twenty miles in a Ponderosa pine forest. The canyon walls on the right bank have a southern exposure showing the basalt layers that make up this large canyon. The northern exposed left bank camouflages the canyon walls with denser stands of forest. This first twenty-mile section has public easement for camping and access on the right bank road. There are ample camps on both banks of this section, so campsites are not listed in the time log. Usually the camps are large and forested on benches with easy access from the river. The wide river is relatively shallow, moves at a fast velocity and has rapids of class 1-2 difficulty.

The dividing point on this tour is the concrete bridge at Wrightman Canyon. It is the end of the right bank road and the beginning of the Wrightman Canyon road to Ritter and highway 395. Below this bridge the river begins to flow southwesterly, exposing the canyon to the drier climate as the forest begins to be more open. Both canyon walls show the basalt layers, and they merge with large buttes such as the layered Johnny Cake Butte almost 2,000 feet above the river. Camps in the lower section are shown on the time log, as they are more scarce than in the upper section. The pine trees begin to merge with juniper trees, and irrigated farmland appears near the trip end. This section is through open grazing land without any practical road access except toward Monument.

The old take-out for boaters was on a large gravel bar on the river just before the concrete bridge at Monument. A new improved take-out has been constructed on the right bank just after the concrete highway bridge.

The relatively short boating season and its location makes the North Fork of the John Day River far less crowded than some of Oregon's more popular rivers. The camping, scenic canyon and the twenty or so class two rapids make this tour an excellent choice for anyone seeking an overnight trip of intermediate difficulty.

North Fork John Day

NORTH FORK JOHN DAY RIVER

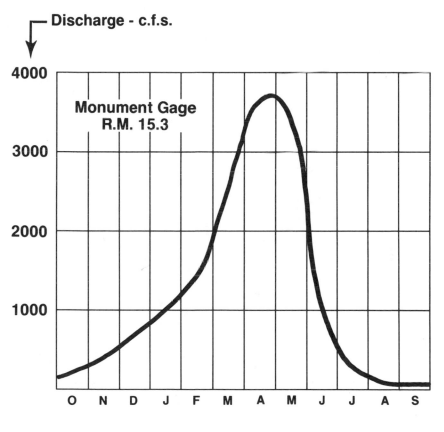

Discharge - c.f.s.

Monument Gage
R.M. 15.3

4000

3000

2000

1000

O N D J F M A M J J A S

Time - Months

SHUTTLE MAP
JOHN DAY AND
NORTH JOHN DAY RIVERS

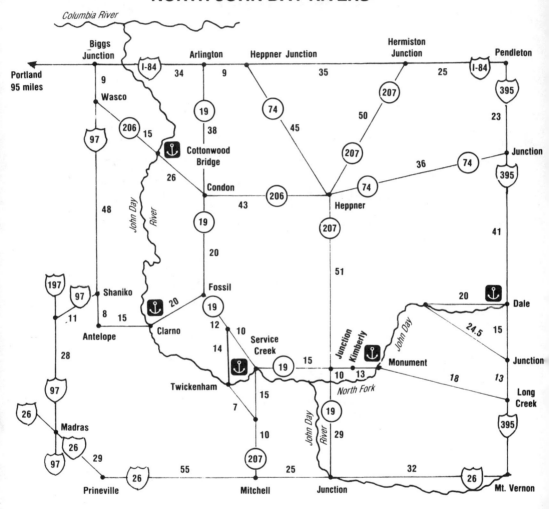

ONE WAY SHUTTLE DISTANCES	Miles	Hours
Dale to Monument	46	1:00
Service Creek to Clarno	42	1:00
Clarno to Cottonwood	66	1:15

North Fork of the John Day River Log

Camas Creek to Monument

River mile: 56.5 to 16.5 .... 40 miles
Drift time: 8 hours 30 minutes .... 4.7 m.p.h.
River slope: 18 feet per mile average
Logged in a raft
River discharge: 2200-2300 c.f.s. Monument gage
Recommended discharge: 2000 to 5000 c.f.s. Monument gage
Information:
    Managed by U. S. Bureau of Land Management
    Prineville District (541) 447-4115
Shuttle information:
    Boyers Cash Store
    Monument, Oregon (541) 934-2290

    Dale Store
    Dale, Oregon (541) 421-3484

    Barbara McCormack
    Dale, Oregon (541) 421-3416

North Fork John Day

RIVER MILE	RIVER TIME	LEFT BANK	RAPIDS	RIGHT BANK	DESCRIPTION
	4:00				
	50				Concrete bridge
	40		2		Potamus Creek right
	30				
RM 40	20				Homestead ranch
	10				
	3:00		2		Long rapid
	50				
	40				Timber girder bridge
RM 45	30				Stoney Creek right
	20				
	10				
	2:00		2		
	50		2		
	40		2		"A" Frame house
RM 50	30		>2		Long rapids
	20		2		
	10		2		
	1:00		2		
	50				
	40		2		Canyon right
	30		2		
	20				Creek right
RM 56	10				Tin shed
	12:00				Launch - Camas Creek

Adequate camps from launch to concrete bridge.

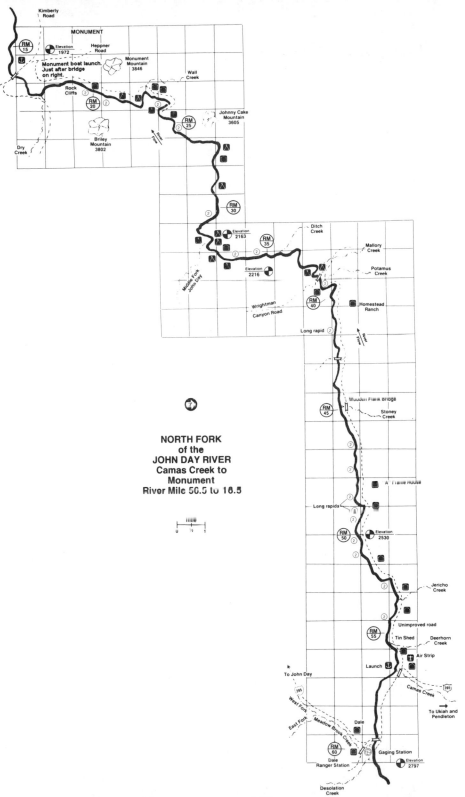

NORTH FORK
of the
JOHN DAY RIVER
Camas Creek to
Monument
River Mile 50.5 to 16.5

RIVER MILE	RIVER TIME	LEFT BANK	RAPIDS	RIGHT BANK	DESCRIPTION
	9:00				
	50				
RM 16	40				
	30		⊏⊐	⚓	Take out just after bridge at monument on right.
	20				
	10	〰			} Irrigated farmland
	8:00			⬠	Rock Cliffs - (river gate)
RM 20	50		• 2 • 1		
	40		• 2		
	30				
	20			⛺	
	10			⛺ 〰	Board Creek
	7:00	⛺		⬠ ⬠	Wall Creek Old ranch buildings
	50		• 2	⛺	
RM 25	40		• 2		Creek right
	30			〰	
	20				
	10		• 1	⛺	
	6:00			⬠	
	50		• 2	⛺	
RM 30	40	Left bank posted no trespassing			
	30		• 2		
	20			⛺	
	10	⛺ 〰		⛺	Middle Fork John Day - left
	5:00			⬠	
	50	⛺			
RM 35	40	⛺	• 2 • 2		
	30			〰	Ditch Creek, right
	20				
	10			>〰	Small Creek, right
	4:00	⛺		〰	Mallory Creek, right

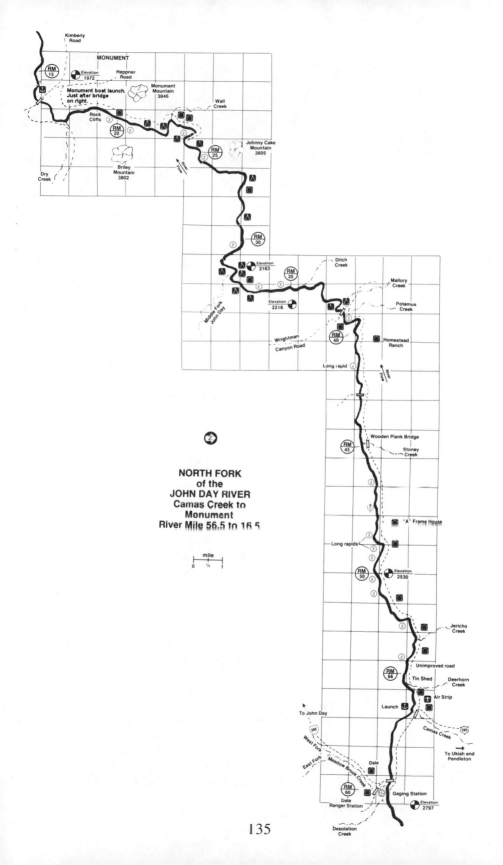

NORTH FORK
of the
JOHN DAY RIVER
Camas Creek to
Monument
River Mile 56.5 to 16.5

Klamath River Powerhouse

Klamath River

John C. Boyle Powerhouse to Copco Lake

The Klamath drainage basin begins in the high plateau Klamath marsh area. Rivers such as the Wood, Sprague and Williamson drain into the connecting Agency and Upper Klamath lakes. A short section called Link River connects Upper Klamath Lake to Lake Ewauna. The Klamath River actually begins at the lower end of Lake Ewauna in the city of Klamath Falls. Ten miles downstream from Klamath Falls is the Keno Dam; nine miles below Keno Dam is the John C. Boyle Dam and another four-and-one-half miles downstream is the John C. Boyle powerhouse. One-half mile below the power house is the launch for this tour.

Because of lakes, reservoirs, dams, flumes, flatwater sections and penstocks there isn't much free-flowing Klamath River whitewater in Oregon. Of the 249 mile Klamath River 209 miles are in California. In Oregon only about five miles below Keno Dam plus eleven miles below the John C. Boyle powerhouse are considered boatable free flowing whitewater. It is the latter eleven mile section, plus another six miles if the boater takes out at Copco Lake, that is the subject of this tour.

For whitewater boaters a potential complication is the proposed Salt Caves hydroelectric project which would essentially eliminate whitewater boating on this eleven mile section of the river. The city of Klamath Falls Salt Caves hydroelectric project has been the focus of a bitterly devisive controversy that rivals earlier dam conflicts in Hells Canyon of the Snake River. The people of Oregon, by initiative petition in 1988, included the controversial section of the Klamath River as a State Scenic Waterway. In 1990 the river was declared eligible for inclusion in the National Wild and Scenic Rivers System. At the request of Governor Barbara Roberts, the Secretary of Interior Bruce Babbitt designated the Klamath River as a Wild and Scenic River in the federal system in 1994. The city of Klamath Falls has filed a lawsuit to overturn the designation. As the political intrigues are acted out, the whitewater boaters can only hope the results will be in favor of a majority of Oregonians who want a free flowing river.

River flows for this eleven mile section of the Klamath River are almost entirely dependent on turbine release from the John C. Boyle powerhouse. The flow in this section from natural sources is about 350 c.f.s. plus 1,250 c.f.s. maximum from each of the two powerhouse turbines. With one turbine operating the total river flow is about 1,500 c.f.s., which is the usual flow during summer months when most boating is done. With two turbines operating usually during winter and

137

spring, the discharge is 3,000 c.f.s. which is considered too difficult for most boaters. This log is for a flow of one turbine.

Although turbine operation causes flows of 1,500 c.f.s. during most of the boating season, there is a period during the summer when turbine operation may be shut down for maintenance. Boaters should check with Pacific Power and Light Company in Portland to verify the flow and period of time that turbines operate (1-800-547-1501). The hydrograph for the mean monthly discharge gives a good estimate of the times of year when one or two turbines operate. Powerplant discharge fluctuates widely on a daily basis between the minimum natural flow and flows with either one or two turbines operating. During the summer single turbine operation usually occurs between 4:00 a.m. and 4:00 p.m., but these times may vary, giving good reason for the boater to confirm powerplant operation prior to a trip.

Within this eleven mile whitewater section, depending on discharge, there are about fourteen class three rapids, three or four class four rapids (Satan's Gate, The Dragon, Ambush, Snag Island Falls), and two class five rapids (Caldera, Hells Corner). Most of these major rapids are within an intense four mile gorge section with steep river slope and rocky channel in the last half of the trip. The Klamath has a reputation for sharp basalt boulders in brown foamy water, making river reading difficult, and it can take its toll on both equipment and on anyone unlucky enough to be swimming through rapids.

The first six miles of the trip enable boaters to become familiar with the brown, fairly fast water and sharp basalt boulders of the Klamath. This section, from the launch (R.M. 220) to Frain Ranch (R.M. 215) has lots of "busy" water, but at one turbine discharge and a flow of 1,500 c.f.s. the rapids difficulty does not exceed class three. The first major rapids is Caldera at Frain Ranch which is the beginning of the four mile gorge section ending at Snag Island Falls rapids (R.M. 211), although rapids continue to the state line take-out (R.M. 209).

The last five mile section of the trip ending at state line is what brings boaters to the Klamath River. The rapids and the fact that the river is runnable throughout the summer when many other rivers lack boatable water are reasons enough to attract boaters. The average river gradient from the launch to state line take-out is forty-nine feet per mile. Some sections within the gorge, depending on where the measuring is done, show river gradients exceeding 80 feet per mile. Add 1,500 c.f.s. to a rocky channel with this gradient, and we have what boaters call Caldera, Satan's Gate, Hells Corner, The Dragon and Ambush.

This Klamath River trip is essentially a day trip but may be divided to include overnight camping. Most of the camps are within the first six miles of the trip, and the Frain Ranch is a popular halfway stopping point. The gorge section does not lend itself to camping, and the section below the state line is private posted land.

Klamath River Camps

River Mile	Name	Left or Right Bank	BLM Designated Camp	Comments
219	Osprey	R		Below Island
218.0		R	•	
217.8		R	•	
217.3		R	•	
217.0		R	•	
216.9		R	•	
216.8		R	•	
216.7		R	•	
216.4		R	•	
215.3	Bull	L		
214.6	Frain Ranch	L		Private Land

The road to the launch for this trip is at road mile 42 on Route 66. There is a sign at this junction (J.C. Boyle Powerplant Road), and the powerplant is 4.5 miles down a gravel road. One-half mile beyond the powerplant is a steep 100 yard long access road to the river launch site. The main road continues downriver another six miles, but it is a low gear road for high clearance vehicles or four wheel drive rigs. This road is used sometimes on overnight trips to carry camping gear to downstream camp sites so the boats do not have to carry equipment on the river.

The preferred shuttle route is via Ashland, Hornbrook, Ager junction to one of three take-out points. The first take-out for the boater is at the state line of Oregon and California (R.M. 209). The boater's clues for this take-out are old log crib piers, the only remains of a former bridge. This is a somewhat difficult take-out, and conventional vehicles may not be able to drive all the way to the river. The second take-out is 5.5 miles downstream from the Oregon-California border take-out at a designated "Access Number One" site (R.M. 203). Access Number One is only 0.6 mile upstream from the main concrete bridge across the river and 0.7 miles upstream from the Copco Lake store take-out. There are six designated access points within five miles upstream from the head of Copco Lake, but only site Number One is for boaters, the rest are for fishermen. Access Number One is a good take-out, but, if the access gate is locked, one must carry equipment about 50 yards to the road and then lift equipment over a gate or fence. This take-out is on the left bank and there are no clearly obvious signs of where it is, so the boater must watch closely. Access Number One is near the head of the lake, so it is three-fourths of a mile of flatwater rowing from there to the third take-out at the Copco Lake store (R.M. 202) immediately below the concrete bridge and on the right or north shore. There is a two dollar per person take-out charge at Copco Lake store.

It is possible to boat only the main rapids of the gorge section by going on the Topsy road upstream from the State line take-out to Frain ranch. This is a difficult section of road, but it does give the option of boating the gorge section twice in a day.

Natural Flow (No turbine discharge)

KLAMATH RIVER

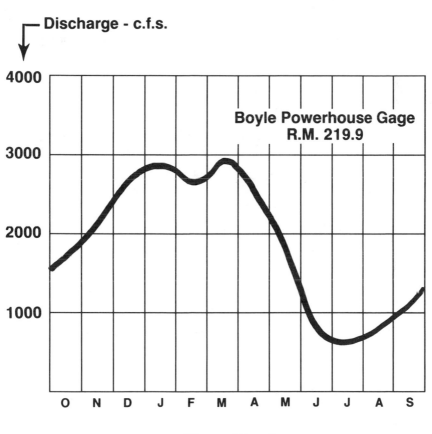

SHUTTLE MAP
KLAMATH RIVER

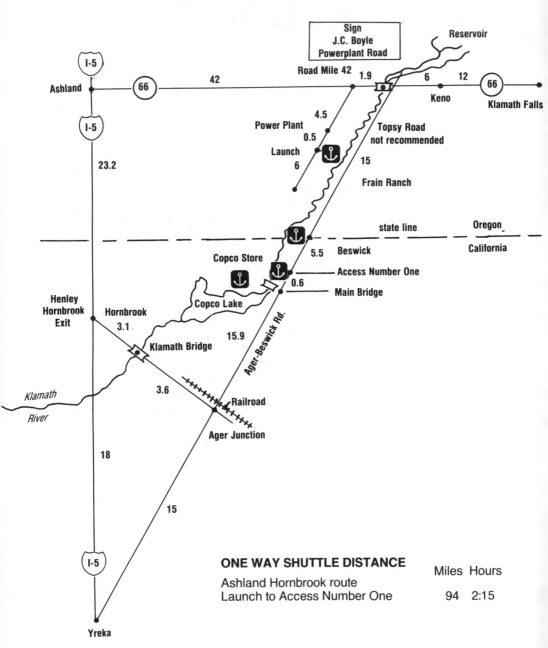

Sign
J.C. Boyle
Powerplant Road

Reservoir

I-5

66

42

Road Mile 42   1.9

6   12

66

Ashland

Keno

Klamath Falls

I-5

4.5

Power Plant

Topsy Road
not recommended

0.5

23.2

Launch

6

15

Frain Ranch

state line

Oregon

California

5.5   Beswick

Copco Store

Access Number One

0.6

Main Bridge

Henley
Hornbrook
Exit

Hornbrook

Copco Lake

3.1

15.9

Klamath Bridge

Ager-Beswick Rd.

Klamath
River

3.6

Railroad

Ager Junction

18

15

I-5

Yreka

ONE WAY SHUTTLE DISTANCE

Ashland Hornbrook route
Launch to Access Number One

Miles Hours

94   2:15

Klamath River Log

John C. Boyle Powerhouse to Copco Lake

River mile: 218.5 to 202 .... 16.5 miles
Drift time: 4 hours 10 minutes .... 2.5 m.p.h.
Logged in raft
River slope: 49 feet per mile average (state line takeout)
River discharge: 1500 c.f.s. (one turbine operating)
Recommended discharge: 1500 c.f.s.
River discharge information:
      Pacific Power and Light Company
      Portland, Oregon
      Toll free recording 1-800-547-1501
Managed by:
      U.S. Bureau of Land Management
      Klamath Falls, OR (541) 883-6916
Car Shuttle:
      Copco Lake Store (916) 459-3655
      The Copco store does not do shuttles but has phone numbers of
      local shuttle drivers.
            Bud Johnson (916) 459-3042
            Bob Perlic (916) 459-5216

RIVER MILE	RIVER TIME	LEFT BANK	RAPIDS	RIGHT BANK	DESCRIPTION
	2:00				
	55		2 / 3		
	50		2 / 2		Island keep left / Island keep left
	45		3 / 3		
	40		4 / 5 5		Island keep left / HELLS CORNER
	35		3 / 3 / 4		
	30		4 / 3		
	25		5		CALDERA
RM 215	20	▲	2	▲	Frain Ranch left / Road to river right
	15				Gage cable
	10	▲		▲	
	5	▲	2		
	1:00		2		Frequent camp area
	55			▲	
	50	▲	2		Road left
	45				
	40			▲	
	35				
	30		2		
	25		2		
	20				
	15	▲	2 / 2		
	10		3	▲	Osprey Island
	5				
RM 220	12:00		2	⚓	BLM Launch

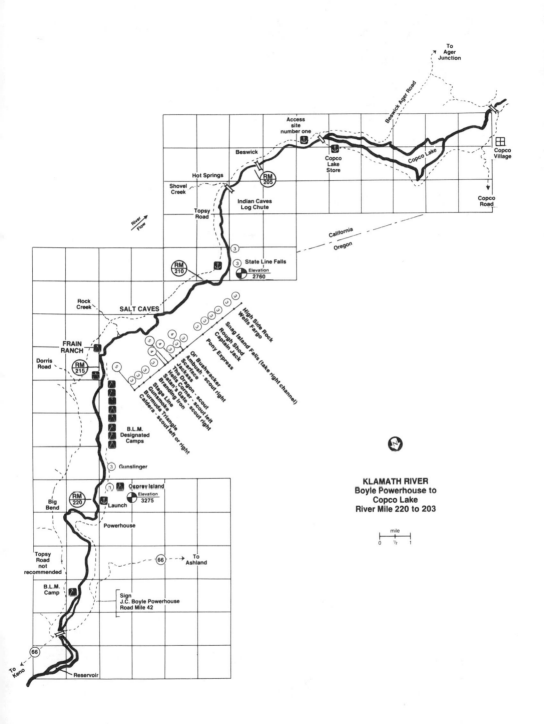

To
Ager
Junction

Beswick Ager Road

Access
site
number one

Beswick

Copco
Lake
Store

Copco Lake

Copco
Village

Hot Springs

RM
205

Shovel
Creek

Topsy
Road

Indian Caves
Log Chute

Copco
Road

River
Flow

California

Oregon

RM
210

State Line Falls

Elevation
2760

Rock
Creek

SALT CAVES

High Side Rock
Wells Fargo
Snag Island Falls (take right channel)
Rough Shod
Captain Jack
Pony Express

FRAIN
RANCH

RM
215

Dorris
Road

Ol' Bushwacker
Ambush - scout right
Scarface
The Dragon - scout left
Satan's Gate - scout right
Hell's Corner
Branding Iron
State Line
Gunsmoke
Gunsmoke Triangle
Burnside
Caldera - scout left or right

B.L.M.
Designated
Camps

Gunslinger

Osprey Island

Elevation
3275

Big
Bend

RM
220

Launch

Powerhouse

Topsy
Road
not
recommended

B.L.M.
Camp

66

To
Ashland

Sign
J.C. Boyle Powerhouse
Road Mile 42

To
Keno

66

Reservoir

KLAMATH RIVER
Boyle Powerhouse to
Copco Lake
River Mile 220 to 203

mile
0   ½   1

RIVER MILE	RIVER TIME	LEFT BANK	RAPIDS		RIGHT BANK	DESCRIPTION
	10	⚓				Take out - Access number one
	5					
	4:00					
	55		1			
	50					
	45					
RM 205	40	🏠	2			Bridge
	35		1			
	30		1 1			
	25	🏠	1	⊙		Island, keep left
	20					Bridge
	15			1		Weir
	10			2		Flume, right
	5	🏠				
	3:00		⊙	2 2		Island, both channels shallow
	55			2		Weir
	50			2		Weir
	45			2		
	40			2		
	35	⚓	3 3			Weir Weir State Line takeout Weir
RM 210	30		⊙	2		Island, keep right
	25		3	3		Cable trolley
	20		3			
	15		⊙	3		Island, keep right
	10		3 3			Long rapids
	5		3 3			
	2:00		3	2		

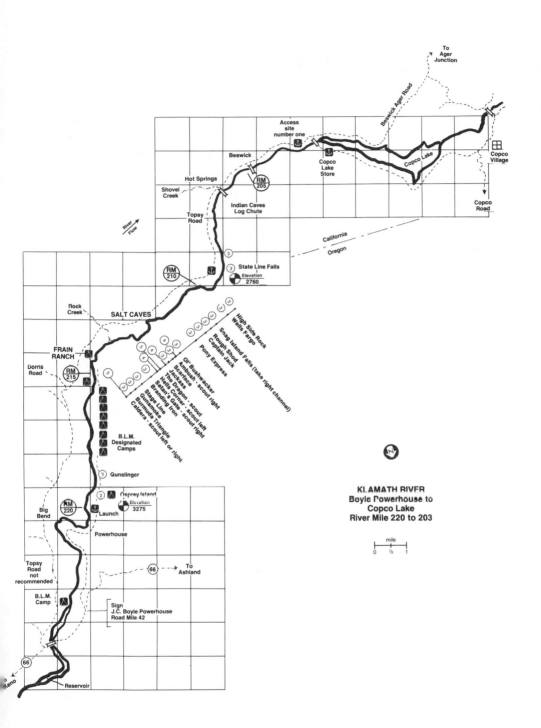

To
Ager
Junction

Beswick Ager Road

Access
site
number one

Beswick

Copco Lake

Copco
Lake
Store

Copco
Village

Hot Springs

RM
205

Shovel
Creek

Indian Caves
Log Chute

Topsy
Road

Copco
Road

River Flow

California

Oregon

RM
210

State Line Falls

Elevation
2760

Rock
Creek

SALT CAVES

High Side Rock
Wells Fargo
Snag Island Falls (take right channel)
Rough Shod
Captain Jack
Pony Express
Ol' Bushwacker - scout right
Ambush
Scarface
Jackass
The Dragon - scout right
Hell's Corner - scout left
Satan's Gate
Branding Iron
Stage Line - scout right
Gunsmoke
Bermuda Triangle
Caldera - scout left or right

FRAIN
RANCH

Dorris
Road

RM
215

B.L.M.
Designated
Camps

Gunslinger

Osprey Island

Elevation
3275

Big
Bend

RM
220

Launch

Powerhouse

Topsy
Road
not
recommended

66

To
Ashland

B.L.M.
Camp

Sign
J.C. Boyle Powerhouse
Road Mile 42

66

Keno

Reservoir

KLAMATH RIVER
Boyle Powerhouse to
Copco Lake
River Mile 220 to 203

mile
0   ½   1

McKenzie River

Blue Lake to Leaburg Dam

The McKenzie River is one of Oregon's most popular driftboating rivers. Its scenery and fishing reputation have long been famous, and a specially designed drift boat bears its name. The river is in the back yard of one of Oregon's major metropolitan areas and receives heavy use year around. The flow of the McKenzie is regulated by Smith River reservoir, Cougar Lake and Blue River Lake. The river has its origins in the Cascade mountain range at Clear Lake. From there it flows 91 miles westerly, through a forested valley typical of the Cascades, to its confluence with the Willamette River. There are many cabins along the river but, for the most part, boaters have a sense of isolation because of the forested banks.

Most of the entire length of the McKenzie River is boatable. The log in this book covers the most commonly used section from the community of Blue River to the backwaters of Leaburg Dam, a distance of 18 miles. Boaters also boat from Olallie Campground, about twenty-three river miles upstream from Blue River. The rapids difficulty in both sections is about the same, class two and three at moderate flows, but the river gradient, river velocity and frequency of rapids is much greater in the section above Blue River. Also, the river flow (c.f.s.) is much less in the upper section than at the Vida gaging station.

A popular play spot for kayakers is an "endo" hole and surfing wave at a log scaling station at road mile 43 between Blue River and McKenzie Bridge. Another play spot is called "Browns Hole", at river mile 46 in the log.

The highly regulated dam controlled flows of the McKenzie River mean the water is clear and cold. One advantage of this regulation is that the river section in this log is boatable year around. In late summer, when most boaters are searching for rivers with sufficient water to boat, the people near the McKenzie can confidently enjoy this excellent river.

McKENZIE RIVER

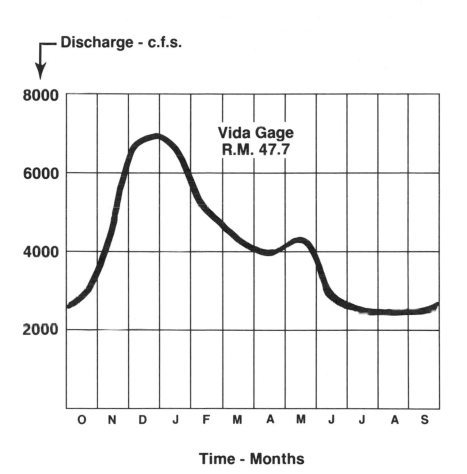

Discharge - c.f.s.

Vida Gage
R.M. 47.7

Time - Months

McKenzie River Log

Blue River to Leaburg Dam

River mile: 57.5 to 39.8 .... 18 miles
Drift time: 4 hours .... 4.5 m.p.h.
Logged in McKenzie drift boat
River slope: 16 feet per mile average
River discharge: 4,250 c.f.s. Coburg gage
Recommended discharge: 1,500 to 5,000 c.f.s. Vida gage
River discharge information:
    National Weather Service
    (503) 261-9246

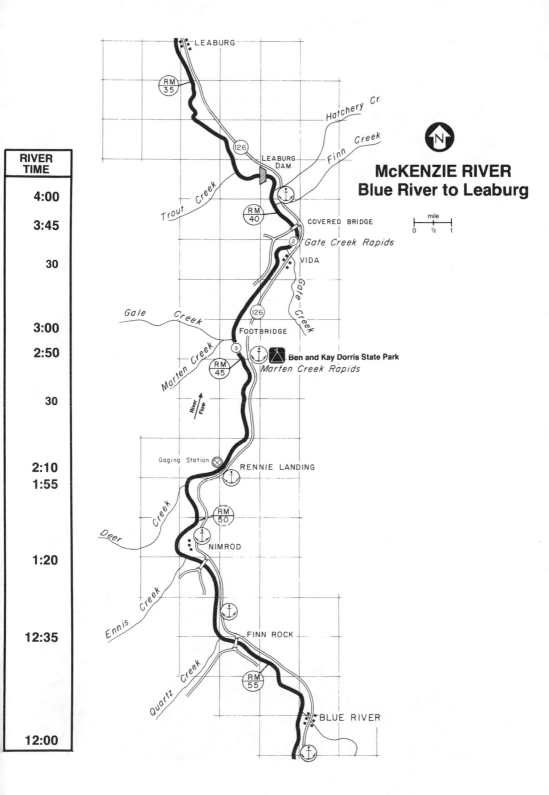

RIVER TIME

4:00

3:45

30

3:00
2:50

30

2:10
1:55

1:20

12:35

12:00

N

**McKENZIE RIVER
Blue River to Leaburg**

mile
0   ½   1

LEABURG

RM 35

Hatchery Cr.

126

Finn Creek

LEABURG DAM

Trout Creek

RM 40

COVERED BRIDGE

2   Gate Creek Rapids

VIDA

Gale Creek

Gale   Creek

126

FOOTBRIDGE

Marten Creek

3

Ben and Kay Dorris State Park

RM 45   Marten Creek Rapids

River Flow

Gaging Station ⊗

RENNIE LANDING

Creek

RM 50

Deer

NIMROD

Ennis Creek

FINN ROCK

Quartz Creek

RM 55

BLUE RIVER

Metolius River

Metolius River

Lower 99 Bridge to Camp Monty

Just north of Sisters, Oregon, and near Black Butte is one of Oregon's most scenic areas. In a small valley springs rise to form the headwaters of the Metolius River. This has long been a popular camping area in one of Oregon's largest remaining stands of ancient ponderosa pine forests. The area is a premier fly fishing domain that also lends itself to hiking, biking, cross country skiing and whitewater boating. The crown jewel in the recreational tiara is the Metolius River. The uniqueness of the Metolius was confirmed in 1988 when it received recognition under the State Rivers Initiative legislation and the federal Omnibus Rivers Bill placing it under Wild and Scenic Rivers protection.

This clear blue fast-moving and cold river runs about eleven miles through a forested camp and semi-developed area to Lower Bridge 99 at the end of the paved road paralleling the river. This upper eleven miles include three low bridges and numerous fishermen, suggesting that the Lower Bridge is a good place to start a whitewater tour. A primitive gravel road continues downstream on the right bank another eight miles, but the river starts to become remote below the Lower Bridge. This whitewater tour is a seventeen mile section from Lower Bridge 99 to Camp Monty just before the Metolius empties into Lake Billy Chinook.

The river has a relatively constant width between 50-100 feet, and it moves at a velocity of 5-6 miles per hour the entire trip. The river is shallow with a rocky channel and constant steep slope creating over thirty long and frequent class two rapids, and four class three rapids. In some sections the rapids blend together in almost continuous whitewater. There are factors to consider other than rapids that create hazards. The river is a cold 45°F year around suggesting need for a dry suit even in July. The banks are dense brush, with logs paralleling the bank, sometimes angling into the river and occasionally completely across the river channel. Near Whitewater River at river mile 18 are log jams formed on river bends that could be a boating hazard. This is also the area where two of the four class three rapids occur. There are few good eddies and no sandy beaches for lunch or rest stops. The brush obscures the left bank sidestreams making it difficult to know ones location, so time is the best method of navigating the Metolius. In a more positive vein there are no large river holes and few huge rocks to "wrap" a raft on. Without the log hazards, this would be an intense class two run with four class three rapids thrown in for good measure. The Metolius has a relatively constant flow of 1300-1600 c.f.s. year around. Flow is measured at the gage near Camp Monty at the end of the trip. Flows at the trip beginning are about half those at the gage.

Although the boater must concentrate on manuevering and watching for logs in this fast moving Metolius River, there is always a chance to see mergansers, king fishers, herons, an eagle or the many osprey in the canyon. The boater can get occasional glimpses of the basalt canyon rims near the last section of the trip or "Castle Rocks" on the right bank near river mile 23. While viewing the scenery, pay attention to clues for Camp Monty which is easy to miss. The camp is immediately past the right bank gage house which is also a good takeout point, and directly across from a 600 foot high basalt butte on the left bank. Missing Camp Monty means paddling on the lake about two miles to a private moorage or about 4½ miles to Camp Perry South launch.

The most direct shuttle route, Pioneer Ford, is a 23 mile, hour and fifteen minute drive over gravel roads. This route may be blocked by snow, sometimes until June. The Indian Ford and Sisters-Redmond routes are shuttle alternates. Shuttle drivers should note that Camp Monty and Monty Guard Station are different locations.

METOLIUS RIVER

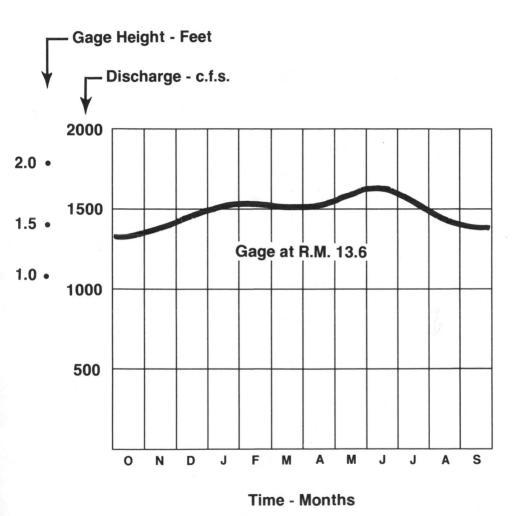

Gage Height - Feet

Discharge - c.f.s.

Gage at R.M. 13.6

Time - Months

SHUTTLE MAP
METOLIUS RIVER

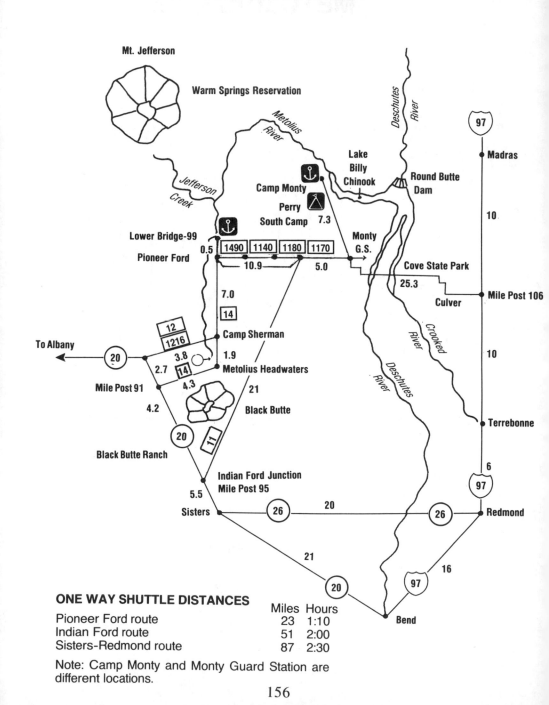

ONE WAY SHUTTLE DISTANCES

	Miles	Hours
Pioneer Ford route	23	1:10
Indian Ford route	51	2:00
Sisters-Redmond route	87	2:30

Note: Camp Monty and Monty Guard Station are different locations.

156

Metolius River Log

Lower Bridge 99 to Camp Monty

River mile: 30 to 13 .... 17 miles
Drift time: 3 hours 25 minutes .... 5.0 m.p.h.
Logged in raft
River slope: 43 feet per mile trip average
River discharge: 1.4 gage near Camp Mounty, 1,360 c.f.s.
Recommended discharge: Boatable throughout year at normal flows.
Information:
    U.S. Forest Service
    Sisters, Oregon
    The river discharge is not a regular part of the National Weather Service information. The relatively constant flow is 1,300-1,600 c.f.s. throughout the year. There are no regular commercial shuttle services available.

RIVER MILE	RIVER TIME	LEFT BANK	RAPIDS	RIGHT BANK	DESCRIPTION
RM 20	2:00				
	55		• 2		Driftwood, left bank
			• 2		Road, right bank
	50				"Castle Rocks" right
	45		• 2		Overhead tree "leaner", left bank
	40				
	35			🏠	
	30		• 2	🏠	Cabins
	25		• 2		
	20				
	15		• 2		
	10		•>2		
	5		•>2		
	1:00				
	55				
	50				
RM 25	45		•>2		
	40				
	35		• 2		
	30	～～～	• 2		
	25		2 / 2		
	20	～～～ ⛺	•>3		Jefferson Creek
	15	～～～	• 2		
	10		• 2		
	5		• 2		
RM 30	12:00		⊏⊐	⚓	Bridge 99 - Launch

158

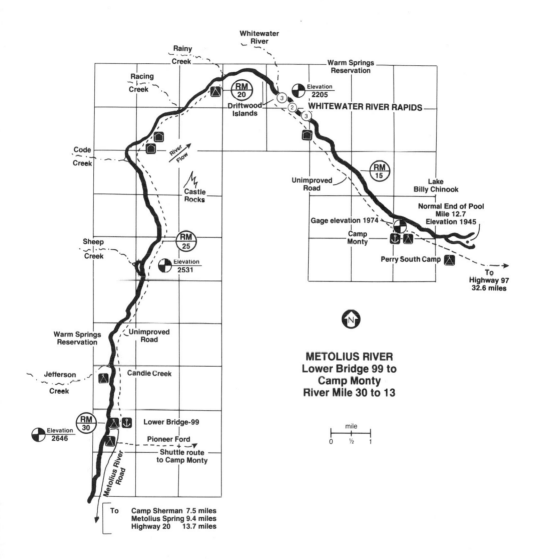

Whitewater
River

Rainy
Creek

Racing
Creek

Warm Springs
Reservation

RM
20

Elevation
2205

Driftwood
Islands

3

2

3

WHITEWATER RIVER RAPIDS

Code
Creek

River
Flow

Castle
Rocks

Unimproved
Road

RM
15

Lake
Billy Chinook

Normal End of Pool
Mile 12.7
Elevation 1945

Gage elevation 1974

Sheep
Creek

RM
25

Elevation
2531

Camp
Monty

Perry South Camp

To
Highway 97
32.6 miles

Warm Springs
Reservation

Unimproved
Road

N

METOLIUS RIVER
Lower Bridge 99 to
Camp Monty
River Mile 30 to 13

Jefferson

Creek

Candle Creek

RM
30

Elevation
2646

Lower Bridge-99

Pioneer Ford

Shuttle route
to Camp Monty

Metolius River
Road

mile

0   ½   1

To   Camp Sherman 7.5 miles
      Metolius Spring 9.4 miles
      Highway 20   13.7 miles

159

RIVER MILE	RIVER TIME	LEFT BANK	RAPIDS	RIGHT BANK	DESCRIPTION
	4:00				
	55				
	50				
	45				
	40				
	35				
	30				
	25			⛺ ⚓	Camp Monty
	20			🏠	Gage House right (Good take out)
RM 15	15		• 2		"Headwall" rapids
	10		• 2		
	5		• 2		
	3:00		• 2		
	55		• 2		
	50		• 2 / 3	🏠	Cabin with blue roof
	45		• 2 / •>2		Log across river
	40				Osprey nest left
	35		• 2		
	30		• 3 / 2		Log across river
	25		• 2 / • 3		WHITEWATER RIVER RAPIDS
	20		⊙		Island - driftwood
	15				Driftwood left and right
	10				Driftwood left
RM 20	5				"Leaner" tree left / Osprey nest left
	2:00			⛺	Primitive camp (lunch stop)

160

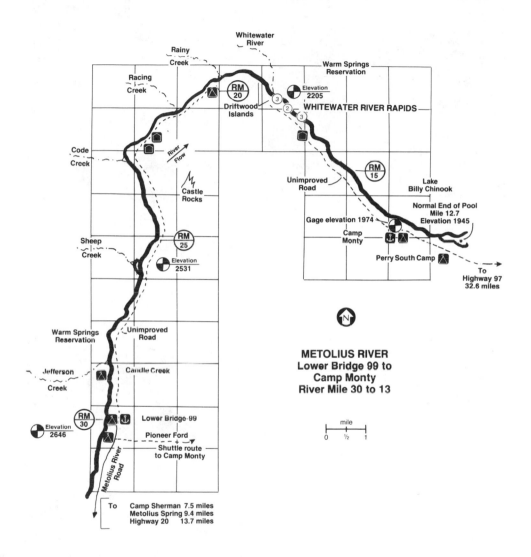

Whitewater
River

Rainy
Creek

Racing
Creek

Warm Springs
Reservation

RM
20

Elevation
2205

Driftwood
Islands

3

2

3

WHITEWATER RIVER RAPIDS

Code
Creek

River
Flow

Castle
Rocks

Unimproved
Road

RM
15

Lake
Billy Chinook

Normal End of Pool
Mile 12.7
Elevation 1945

Gage elevation 1974

Camp
Monty

Sheep
Creek

RM
25

Elevation
2531

Perry South Camp

To
Highway 97
32.6 miles

Warm Springs
Reservation

Unimproved
Road

METOLIUS RIVER
Lower Bridge 99 to
Camp Monty
River Mile 30 to 13

Jefferson
Creek

Candle Creek

RM
30

Elevation
2646

Lower Bridge 99

Pioneer Ford

Shuttle route
to Camp Monty

mile

0   ½   1

Metolius River
Road

To   Camp Sherman 7.5 miles
Metolius Spring 9.4 miles
Highway 20   13.7 miles

Minam Lodge

Minam River

Minam Lodge to the Mouth

The Minam River is located in the Eagle Cap Wilderness beginning at Minam Lake at the base of the Wallowa Mountains which tower up to 9845 feet. This 48 mile river is a State Scenic Waterway and is also a federally designated Wild and Scenic River. The Minam River is one of Oregon's most remote rivers. This tour begins at the Minam Lodge at Red's Horse Ranch. There are no roads to the Minam Lodge, so the only access is by hiking, by horse packing seven miles from the Moss Spring trailhead or from Minam on the right bank trail paralleling the river, or by airplane. The rustic Minam Lodge and its surrounding cabins have long been a famous hunting destination, and only in recent years have a few river runners begun to use the lodge as a base for a wilderness river trip.

The river tour is a twenty-two mile trip within a densely forested canyon that ends at the community of Minam at the river's confluence with the Wallowa River. Many Oregon boaters begin the popular Grande Ronde River trip on the Wallowa River at Minam, but few have seen the Minam River except at its confluence with the Wallowa.

As a practical matter this Minam River tour must begin with some pre-planning, usually resulting in flying boaters and equipment to the Minam Lodge from the airport at LaGrande or Enterprise. Rafts with breakdown frames, inflatable kayaks and hard shell kayaks can be flown into the launch. Hard shell kayakers must check with the air service in advance as they require special loading. Two Perception Dancers and one passenger can, with ingenuity, fit into a Cessna 206. There is a landing fee for the private runway at the Minam Lodge, which is waived if boaters patronize the lodge, so a good plan is to have the excellent lodge breakfast before launch. Breakfast is a bargain, but reservations are required. Communications at the lodge are somewhat sporadic; boaters must call High Country Outfitters in Joseph, Oregon, and hope the reservation gets radioed to the lodge.

The Minam River tour is essentially a day trip. With any luck boaters can launch by 10:00 a.m. and be at the confluence at a reasonable time in the afternoon. With cooperation from the weather, this would be an excellent overnight tour. The tour begins at an elevation of 3600 feet and ends at 2540 feet. During May and June when the river is usually run, the weather can be inclement to say the least. Since few boaters run the Minam, there should be little or no competition for the adequate good camps available.

From LaGrande or Enterprise the flight into Red's Horse Ranch is a short one. The plane climbs over the mountain ridges and drops into the Minam River Canyon, then circles once to check for elk on the runway before dropping down onto the gravel landing strip. The plane is met by lodge personnel with a tractor which hauls river gear to the launch. If the lodge didn't get the word on your breakfast reservation, they will still see that you don't start a river trip on an empty stomach. These are good folks who know what breakfast is all about.

The downstream tour begins in a wooded valley on a clear river with a shallow and relatively uniformly steep slope. There is need to be constantly alert for trees in this fast flowing river. The shallow water means boaters must be constantly manuevering. At low flows, below about 2.2 feet on the Minam gage (800 c.f.s.), the trip can be a rock dodging, boat dragging chore. At higher flows, the river is fast moving with long, continuous rapids. The Minam gage is not a part of the National Weather Service recording. The river flow can only be obtained directly from the gage. On our trip we shuttled vehicles to Minam the day before the trip and checked the gage height. The gage house is visible from Minam and has a split gage, the upper gage on the upriver side of the gage house and the lower gage on the downriver side.

At river mile 18 there is a class three rapids that blends into continuous class two rapids for almost three miles. At river mile 15 there is a noticeable change in slope, and the river continues for another two miles as continuous class one, and two rapids. Slowly, near river mile 12, the river rapids again change and are mainly class one with an occasional class two. The Minam is not a pool and drop river, but rather a fast moving river with constant or frequent rapids that form over the rocky channel. Near river mile 8 the channel widens, and the canyon opens from the dense evergreen forest.

Near river mile 5 the boater may see a right bank road, a log bridge and ranch, but odds are that the boater will not see another party on the river. There are very few whitewater tours in Oregon as remote as the Minam River. This tour can easily be coupled with a Grande Ronde River trip, thus combining two of the best river trips in northeastern Oregon.

MINAM RIVER

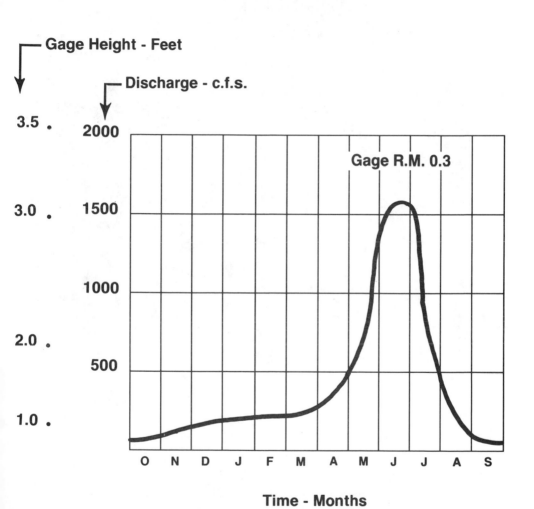

Gage Height - Feet

Discharge - c.f.s.

Gage R.M. 0.3

Time - Months

Minam River

Minam River Log

Minam Lodge to Mouth

River mile: 22 to 0 .... 22 miles
Drift time: 4 hours 15 minutes .... 5.2 m.p.h.
Logged in raft
River slope: 48 feet per mile trip average
River discharge: 1170 c.f.s. Minam gage (2.7 feet gage)
Recommended discharge: 800 c.f.s. minimum (2.2 feet gage)
    Preferable discharge over 2.7 feet.
River discharge information: available only at gage, river mile 0.3
Car shuttle:
    Minam Motel
    Minam, Oregon
    (503) 437-4475

Additional information:
    Spence Air Service
    P.O. Box 217
    Enterprise, OR 97828
    (541) 426-3288

    LaGrande Aviation
    60175 Pierce Road
    LaGrande, OR 97850
    (541) 963-6572

    Minam Lodge — High Country Outfitters
    P. O. Box 26
    Joseph, OR 97846
    (541) 432-9171

RIVER MILE	RIVER TIME	LEFT BANK	RAPIDS	RIGHT BANK	DESCRIPTION
	20				
0 10'	10	⚓	⊐⊏		Minam Launch Confluence Wallowa River
	4:00				
	50				Island
	40				
	30		⊐⊏	⬠	Log bridge Island Ranch
RM 5	20				Island
	10				Island
	3:00				Road, right bank Island
	50				
	40				Island - Canyon opens
RM 10	30		• 2	〜〜〜	Trout Creek
	20		• 2		
	10			〜〜〜	Murphy Creek
	2:00				
	50		• 2 • 2		Island
	40				
	30				Continuous class 1-2 section
RM 15	20				
	10		• 2		Little Minam River
	1:00		• 2		Continuous class 2 section
	50				
	40		• 3		Beginning long rapids section
	30		• 2		
RM 20	20			〜〜〜	Horse Basin Creek
	10		• 2 • 2	〜〜〜	Horseheaven Creek
	12:00	⚓			Launch - Minam Lodge

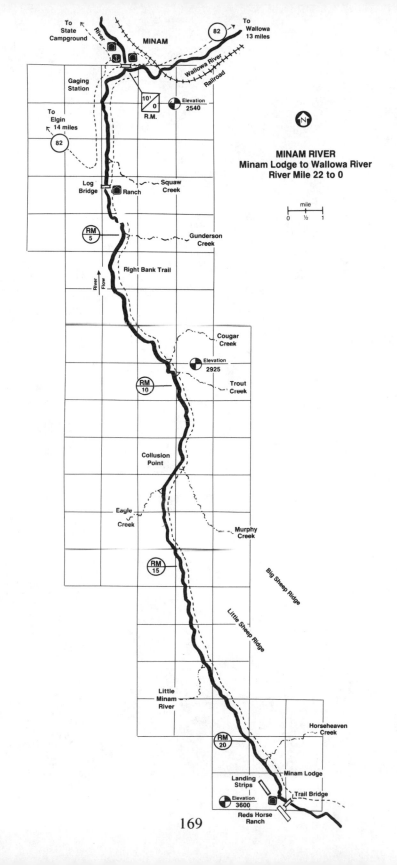

Molalla River

Molalla River

River Mile 35 Bridge to Feyrer Park

The Molalla River is a western Cascade mountain river that is part of the Willamette River drainage. This is a blue-green rain river that flows through a narrow forested canyon. For the most part this relatively small river has boatable flows through the winter and May.

Since there are no formal reporting gages on the Molalla available from the National Weather Service, boaters rely on a staff gage attached to the bridge pier at Feyrer Park for recommended boating periods. Past records of a discontinued gage at R.M. 32.5 near the launch can be used in estimating the magnitude and time certain flows may be expected.

The most popular whitewater day trip on the Molalla is an eight mile canyon section from a bridge at river mile 35 to the community of Glen Avon at river mile 26.6. Local boaters sometimes call this the "Three Bears" section because of the three short drops on one of the rapids near Bear Creek. In this log the trip is extended through a wider valley section to Feyrer Park for a total of 15 miles. At recommended river flows this is essentially a class three run, but it can easily increase in difficulty at high flow.

From the launch just upstream from the bridge, near river mile 35, the boater is immediately in class one-two water. The first major class three rapids at R.M. 34 is only one-half mile below the bridge. This rapids is followed within another half mile by Columnar rapids at R.M. 33.4, which is a quick succession of short drops leading into a quarter-mile long narrow canyon chute of columnar basalt. The steel girder bridge at R.M. 31.6 is the warning for the next class three rapids at R.M. 31.3. All three of these rapids can be viewed from the road.

At river mile 27.5, only a mile upstream from the Glen Avon bridge, is potentially the most difficult rapids on the trip. This rapids should definitely be scouted, since it is on a right bend with a large boulder at the bottom. There is always the possibility for logs in the river on this long narrow sharp curve. At a flow of 3.8 on the Feyrer gage this rapids was a technical class three.

Some boaters take out at the Glen Avon bridge, but the seven mile trip to Feyrer Park is a worthwhile extension of the trip. Downstream from Glen Avon the valley widens with class two rapids, islands and houses visible from the river. There are rapids to surf, and the relatively steep river slope means the river moves along quickly. Don't miss the Molalla in early spring.

MOLALLA RIVER

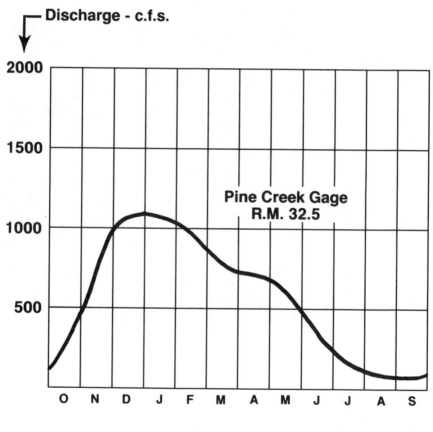

Discharge - c.f.s.

Pine Creek Gage
R.M. 32.5

Time - Months

Molalla River Log

River mile 35 bridge to Feyrer Park

River mile: 35 to 20 .... 15 miles
Drift time: 3 hours .... 5 m.p.h.
Logged in kayak
River slope: 35 feet per mile average
River discharge: 3.8 feet — Feyrer Park bridge
Recommended discharge: 3.0-4.5 feet (3.8 optimum) Feyrer Park bridge gage.

Molalla River

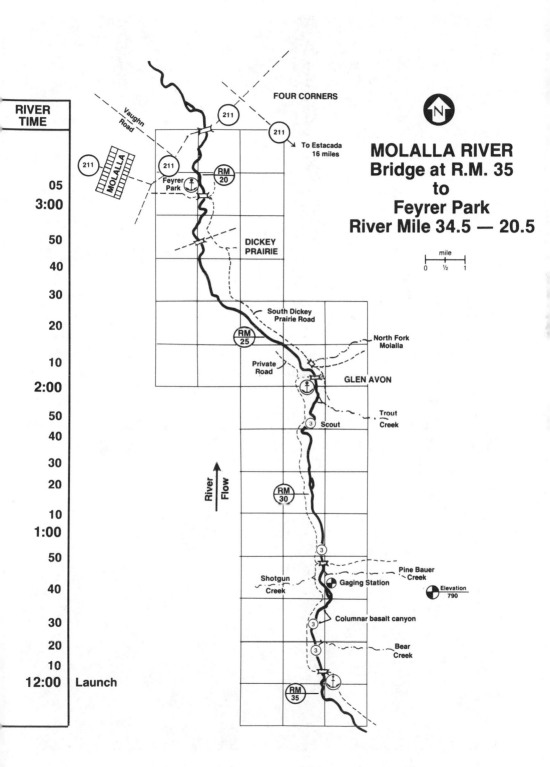

MOLALLA RIVER
Bridge at R.M. 35
to
Feyrer Park
River Mile 34.5 — 20.5

FOUR CORNERS

To Estacada
16 miles

DICKEY
PRAIRIE

South Dickey
Prairie Road

North Fork
Molalla

Private
Road

GLEN AVON

Trout
Creek

Scout

Pine Bauer
Creek

Shotgun
Creek

Gaging Station

Columnar basalt canyon

Bear
Creek

Elevation
790

RIVER
TIME

05
3:00
50
40
30
20
10
2:00
50
40
30
20
10
1:00
50
40
30
20
10
12:00 Launch

River
Flow

MOLALLA

Feyrer
Park

Vaughn
Road

mile
0   ½   1

Owyhee River — R.M. 161

Middle Owyhee River

Three Forks to Rome

The Owyhee River has its origins in the semi-arid high desert Owyhee uplands of Nevada. It courses briefly through a short section of southwestern Idaho before it winds its way through southeastern Oregon, seeking its confluence with the Snake River near Ontario, Oregon. For whitewater boaters the river is divided into three sections: from its source near the Duck Valley Indian Reservation to Three Forks, from Three Forks to Rome and from Rome to the Owyhee Lake reservoir. These sections are referred to as the Upper, Middle and Lower Owyhee. Very few boaters float the upper section. Use increases in the middle section, and by far the most use is in the lower section. This log is for the middle, Three Forks to Rome, section.

Access to Three Forks is a single lane thirty-five mile, dirt and gravel road from highway 95 to the launch. The road meanders from 4,000 to 5,000 feet elevation through a sagebrush and grazing area plateau to the canyon rim near Three Forks. Then it drops over 800 feet to the Three Forks launch where the North Fork, Middle Fork and main Owyhee rivers merge. The road is suitable for pickups and four-wheel-drive vehicles but is generally considered to be a poor choice for conventional automobiles, particularly when wet. Shuttles can be arranged to take equipment and boaters to the launch, leaving the boaters' vehicles at Rome. The thirty-five mile gravel road section takes about one hour and 20 minutes through range land and occasionally through a herd of antelope or deer.

The river trip begins in a wide canyon and flatwater, but it is only 30 minutes, or 1½ miles, to Ledge Rapids which is one of the four major rapids on the trip. Scout Ledge on the left to look at the first ledge drop, followed by 150 yards of rock dodging for the boaters' introduction to Owyhee whitewater. For the next six miles, or roughly two hours of river time, the river is again mostly flatwater. Then the river picks up with some class two rapids in a pool and drop section typical of this river. One of the exceptions to pool and drop is Half Mile Rapids near river mile 151. The boater recognizes this rapids by what appears to be a large earth dam. The river forms a long "S" turn through a constant rock garden paralleling the face of this natural feature. Scout Half Mile on the left. At the end of Half Mile is a pool with a camp on the right followed immediately by Raft Flip Rapids.

At river mile 149 is a large rock that almost entirely blocks the river. This class three rapids is a landmark for Bombshelter Drop at river mile 147. Bombshelter is preceded by Subtle Hole, and both of these rapids, spaced within 100 yards, should be scouted by first-time

177

Ledge Rapids — R.M. 160

Widowmaker Rapids — R.M. 142

Widowmaker Rapids — R.M. 142

boaters. Immediately after Bombshelter rapids is a cave on the left which is a popular camp for boaters.

At river mile 145 is a camp and five boulders across the river, giving this class two rapids the name of Sharkstooth, called Finger Rapids by some boaters. Scout on the left to determine which route to take. This section is within a narrow inner canyon with vertical walls, perhaps four hundred feet high, and outer rims approaching 1,000 feet in vertical elevation. Soldier Creek at river mile 143 is an easily identifiable sidestream and canyon on the right bank, providing the only practical camps in the area. These land marks also orient the boater to his location in respect to Widowmaker which is only 1½ miles downstream from Soldier Creek.

A class three rapids, and two class two rapids are in the seventy five yard entry section preceeding Widowmaker rapids. This entry section should be scouted to determine whether it is worth boating the entry rapids in order to reduce the portage or lining work. While a few boaters do run Widowmaker, more boaters line the rapids, which takes two to four hours for rafts. Scout and line, or portage, on the right. Because boaters do occasionally run Widowmaker, there is a tendency to rate it as a class five difficulty rapids. Scout this rapids and decide for yourself.

After the Widowmaker, the steep-walled canyon begins to widen; yet the boater is still within a narrow inner canyon, and for the next seven miles there is a fairly predictable sequence of class two water with an occasional class three pool and drop rapids. This section also has some large camps. At river mile 132 the canyon widens further, and the last rapids, and the end of the canyon, is at river mile 130. For all practical purposes the last seven miles of the trip to the Rome launch is flat water paddling, often against a severe afternoon wind.

The middle Owyhee river section from Three Forks to Rome is one of the most remote and least-used river tours in Oregon. It is a long distance from major metropolitan areas, and that coupled with short seasons, often precludes boating during low water years.

In early spring, when this section is usually run, the boater may, if lucky, encounter sunny 70° temperatures. More likely it will be below freezing every night, coupled with snow, hail and thunderstorms with severe afternoon winds. It's enough to make a person invest in a dry suit. The boater must have the skills to run three of the four major rapids because no one except kayakers would consider portage of rapids such as Half Mile. Rafters who plan to portage or line the major rapids will find this is more of an expedition than a conventional whitewater tour.

The river use on the Owyhee has grown from virtually nothing in the early 1970's to perhaps 500 persons in a good water year. This is not a river that lends itself readily to casual tourist trips. For the present, the Middle Owyhee is used mostly by expert boaters, and, unless there is some change, this 35 miles of the Owyhee will retain its wilderness character. That in itself makes a trip there worth the effort.

OWYHEE RIVER

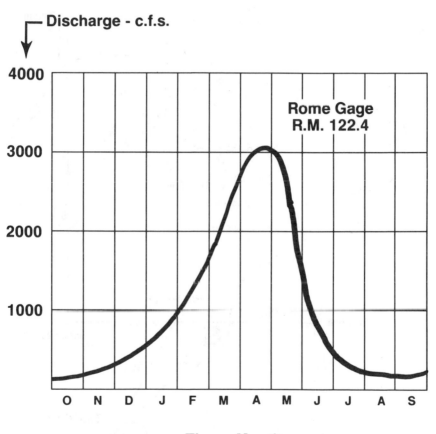

Discharge - c.f.s.

4000

3000

2000

1000

Rome Gage
R.M. 122.4

O N D J F M A M J J A S

Time - Months

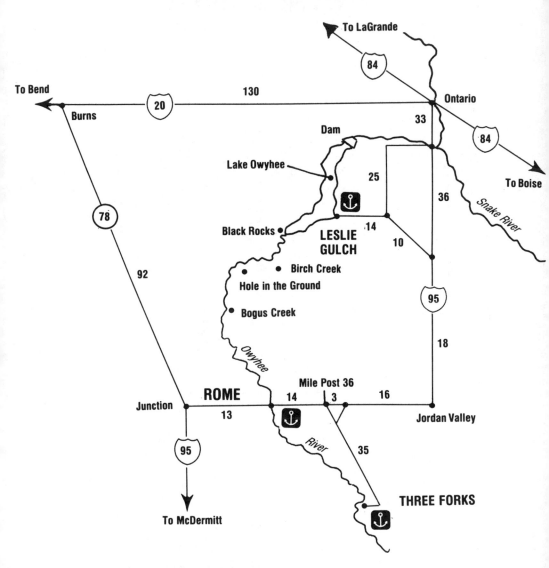

SHUTTLE MAP
OWYHEE RIVER

To LaGrande

84

To Bend

130

20

Burns

33

Ontario

84

To Boise

Dam

Lake Owyhee

25

36

Snake River

Black Rocks

LESLIE GULCH

14

10

78

92

Birch Creek

Hole in the Ground

95

Bogus Creek

18

Owyhee

Mile Post 36

ROME

14

3

16

Junction

13

Jordan Valley

95

River

35

To McDermitt

THREE FORKS

ONE WAY SHUTTLE DISTANCE

	Miles	Hours
Rome to Three Forks	49	1:45
Rome to Leslie Gulch	75	2:30

Jordan Valley is a famous "speed trap" so beware.

182

Middle Owyhee River Log

Three Forks to Rome

River mile: 161 to 126 .... 35 miles
Drift time: 12 hours .... 3 m.p.h.
Logged in raft
River slope: 17 feet per mile, average
River discharge: 1,400 c.f.s. Rome gage
Recommended discharge: 1,000 to 4,000 c.f.s. Rome Gage
River discharge information:
 National Weather Service
 (503) 261-9246
Information: U.S. Bureau of Land Management
Vale District
P.O. Box 700
100 Oregon Street
Vale, OR 97918
(541) 473-3144
Shuttle information:
 Eva Easterday — vehicle shuttle, boat tow
 Jordan Valley, OR 97910
 (541) 586-2352

 Ken Haylett Enterprises — vehicle shuttle, boat tow
 P. O. Box 274
 Jordan Valley, OR 97910
 (208) 459-1292

RIVER MILE	RIVER TIME	LEFT BANK	RAPIDS	RIGHT BANK	DESCRIPTION
	4:00				
	50				
RM 150	40		• 2		
	30			⛺	Raft Flip Drop
	20		• 2		
			• 4		Half Mile Rapids - scout left
	10				
	3:00		• 2		
	50		• 2	⛺	
	40	⛺	• 2		
	30		• 2		
	20		• 2		
	10	⛺		⛺	
		⛺			Deary Pasture Area
RM 155	2:00	~·~·~<		⛺ 🏠	Canyon left Abandoned cabin right
	50				Island — low water
	40		⊙		
	30				
	20			←◯	Spring — Door frame right
	10			>·~·~·~	Canyon
	1:00			⛺ H.W. ⛺ L.W.	Abandoned cabin, right
	50				
	40			⛺	
RM 160	30		• 4		Ledge Rapids - scout left
	20				
	10				
	12:00			⚓	Three Forks Launch

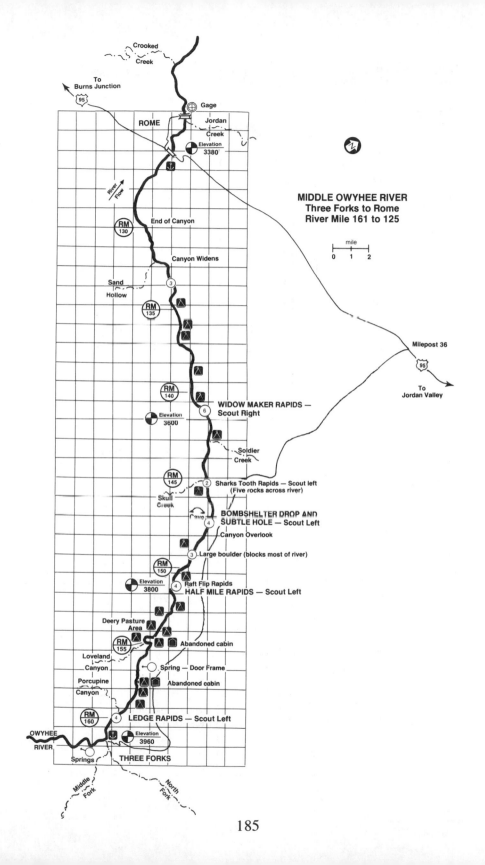

MIDDLE OWYHEE RIVER
Three Forks to Rome
River Mile 161 to 125

185

RIVER MILE	RIVER TIME	LEFT BANK	RAPIDS	RIGHT BANK	DESCRIPTION
	8:00			△s L.W.	
	50		• 2		
	40		• 2		
RM 140	30		• 2 • 2	△ L.W.	
	20		• 2		
	10		• 2 ● 6		Widowmaker - Line or Portage right
	7:00		● 4 • 2		Entry to Widowmaker - scout right
	50		• 2 ● 3		
	40			△ △	Soldier Creek right
	30		⊙		Large camp area
	20				
	10				
	6:00		• 2 • 2		
RM 145	50	△	• 2		Sharks Teeth (Finger Rapids) scout left
	40				
	30		• 2		
	20		• 2		
	10				
	5:00	⌒ cave			
	50		● 4 ● 3		Bombshelter Drop } scout right
	40				Subtle Drop
	30		• 2		
	20	△s			
	10		• 2 • 2		
	4:00		• 2 ● 3		Large rock blocks most of river

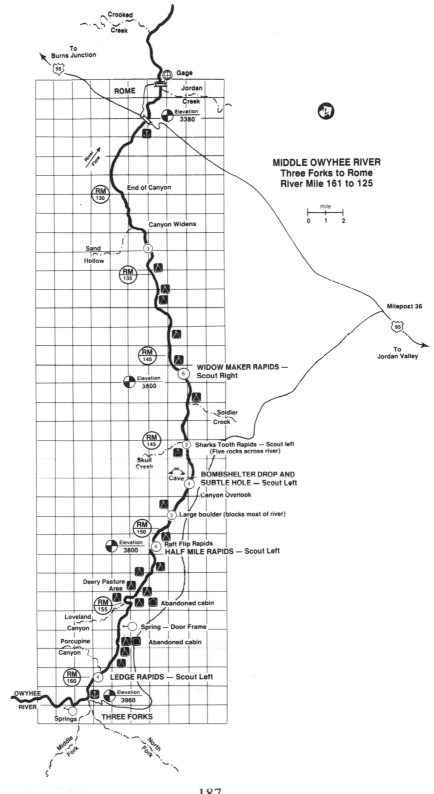

Crooked Creek

To Burns Junction

95

Gage

ROME

Jordan Creek

Elevation 3380'

MIDDLE OWYHEE RIVER
Three Forks to Rome
River Mile 161 to 125

River Flow

RM 130 End of Canyon

Canyon Widens

mile
0   1   2

Sand Hollow

3

RM 135

Milepost 36

95

To Jordan Valley

RM 140

Elevation 3600

6   WIDOW MAKER RAPIDS — Scout Right

Soldier Creek

RM 145

2   Sharks Tooth Rapids — Scout left (Five rocks across river)

Skull Creek

Cave

1   BOMBSHELTER DROP AND SUBTLE HOLE — Scout Left

Canyon Overlook

3   Large boulder (blocks most of river)

RM 150

Elevation 3800

4   Raft Flip Rapids

HALF MILE RAPIDS — Scout Left

Deery Pasture Area

RM 155   Abandoned cabin

Loveland Canyon

Spring — Door Frame

Porcupine Canyon

Abandoned cabin

RM 160   4   LEDGE RAPIDS — Scout Left

OWYHEE RIVER

Elevation 3960

Springs

THREE FORKS

Middle Fork

North Fork

187

RIVER MILE	RIVER TIME	LEFT BANK	RAPIDS	RIGHT BANK	DESCRIPTION
					ROME
	12:00			⚓	BLM — Launch site
	50				
	40				
	30				
	20				
	10				
	11:00				
RM 130	50		2		End of Canyon
	40				
	30				
	20				
	10				Canyon widens
	10:00		2		
	50		2 2		
	40		3 2 2		
	30		2 2		
	20		2 2	⛺	
RM 135	10				
	9:00				
	50			⛺	
	40			⛺	
	30				
	20		2		
	10		2 2		
RM 138	8:00		2	⛺ L.W.	
			2		

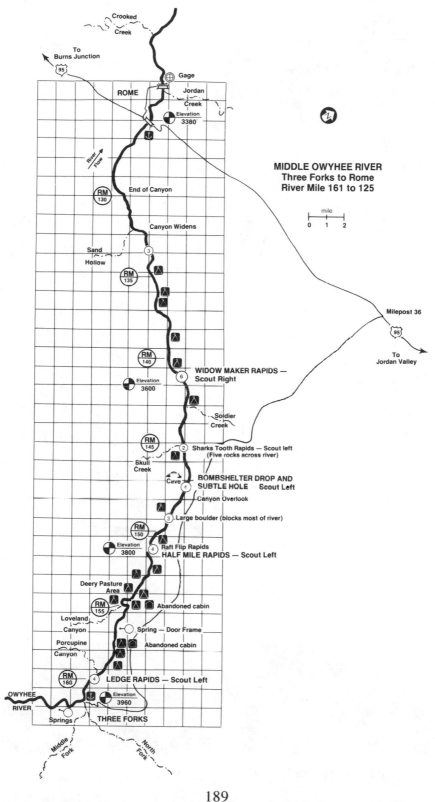

Crooked
Creek

To
Burns Junction

95

Gage

ROME

Jordan
Creek

Elevation
3380'

River Flow

RM 130

End of Canyon

Canyon Widens

Sand
Hollow

3

RM 135

MIDDLE OWYHEE RIVER
Three Forks to Rome
River Mile 161 to 125

mile
0 1 2

Milepost 36

95

To
Jordan Valley

RM 140

Elevation
3600

WIDOW MAKER RAPIDS —
Scout Right

6

Soldier
Creek

RM 145

2 Sharks Tooth Rapids — Scout left
(Five rocks across river)

Skull
Creek

Cave

1

BOMBSHELTER DROP AND
SUBTLE HOLE   Scout Left

Canyon Overlook

3 Large boulder (blocks most of river)

RM 150

Elevation
3800

Raft Flip Rapids

4 HALF MILE RAPIDS — Scout Left

Deery Pasture
Area

RM 155

Abandoned cabin

Loveland
Canyon

Spring — Door Frame

Porcupine
Canyon

Abandoned cabin

RM 160

4 LEDGE RAPIDS — Scout Left

OWYHEE

RIVER

Elevation
3960

Springs

THREE FORKS

Middle
Fork

North
Fork

189

Greeley Cabin Hot Springs Camp — R.M. 77

Lower Owyhee River

Rome to Leslie Gulch

The Lower Owyhee River is one of three sections boated by whitewater enthusiasts. The Upper Owyhee is from its source in Nevada to Three Forks, the Middle Owyhee is from Three Forks to Rome and this log for the Lower Owyhee is from Rome to Leslie Gulch on Lake Owyhee. The Lower Owyhee is by far the most used of the three river sections, yet even in a high-use year probably no more than 1,500 persons will boat this remote short-season river tour. During low water years it is not uncommon for no one to boat the Owyhee.

This high plateau area has been inhabited by Indians, Hudson's Bay trappers, Basque sheepherders and wildlife. A short distance from Rome, on Jordan Creek, is the grave of the youngest member of the Lewis and Clark Expedition, Jean Baptiste Charbonneau, 1805-1866, who was less than two-months old when he started the journey on his mother's back. One can see old cabins, petroglyphs and Basque name places in the Owyhee country. The area is close to the Malhuer Wildlife Refuge so migratory fowl are common in spring. It is one of the few places in Oregon where one might see antelope or Big Horn sheep. In spite of the area's reputation for rattlesnakes, I have never encountered any. Perhaps this suggests that sleeping in enclosed tents and exercising normal caution when hiking or scouting rapids reduces the chances for seeing rattlesnakes.

The trip begins at the Bureau of Land Management boat ramp at the highway 95 bridge at Rome. For the first six miles, or two hours of drift time, the boater is in flatwater meandering through irrigated farmland. Near Crooked Creek at river mile 115 the river enters the remote Lower Owyhee Canyon. The total trip is 55 miles to the Owyhee reservoir and then another 10 miles across the reservoir to the Leslie Gulch take out. This is a relatively easy whitewater tour because there are only three class three rapids to contend with: Whistling Bird at river mile 93, Montgomery rapids at river mile 89 and Rock Dam rapids at river mile 83.

For the most part, this is a class three difficulty river section with enough class one and two rapids to keep the trip exciting. The primary concern for boaters is that this remote area means help may be a long distance in case of problems. In addition to a river map which shows only the rapids of class three difficulty, a straight line time log is included. The log gives a better insight into the river characteristics, for, although there are long flatwater sections, the trip does have several rapids sections which are not indicated on the map.

191

Owyhee River near Rome — R.M. 115

Iron Point Canyon — R.M. 89

Rustler Cabin — R.M. 97

Lambert Rocks — R.M. 96

The primary benefits of this trip, in addition to its remoteness, are the wildlife and spectacular geology. Although small scale by comparison to some of the similar geologic areas in Montana, the Dakotas or the Four Corners area of the southwest, this area is unique for Oregon. The combination of ancient sedimentary and volcanic deposits has resulted in an area worthwhile visiting if there were no rapids at all. Rustler cabin, Whistling Bird, Lambert Rocks and the outstanding Iron Point canyon at river mile 89 combine with hot springs and a few great camps to make this a special Oregon river trip.

In former years, it was possible to take out boats at one of the ranches near the lower part of the trip. Presently, boaters may take out before the reservoir only at the BLM Birch Creek Ranch. The shuttle road into the ranch can sometimes be a rugged four-wheel drive trip. Boaters may arrange equipment shuttles from Birch Creek Ranch to the canyon rim or to Jordan Valley. Below Birch Creek Ranch at the beginning of the Owyhee Reservoir the boater has three alternatives. With a four-horsepower motor, four-gallons of gas and four hours, one may motor two large rafts to Leslie Gulch providing there isn't much wind. Boats may also be towed by powerboat in slightly less time, but anyone planning to row or paddle the ten-mile lake section should plan on an entire day. Leslie Gulch is an attractive area in itself, but after the reservoir section, it is anti-climatic to the trip. Reservoirs have never been terribly exciting for whitewater boaters, but the Lower Owyhee Canyon is worthwhile for everyone.

Whistling Bird Rapids — R.M. 94

OWYHEE RIVER

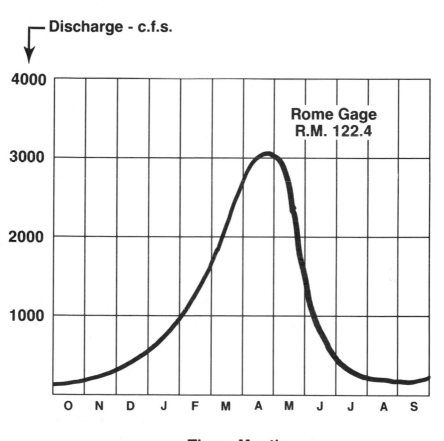

Discharge - c.f.s.

4000

3000

2000

1000

Rome Gage
R.M. 122.4

O N D J F M A M J J A S

Time - Months

SHUTTLE MAP
OWYHEE RIVER

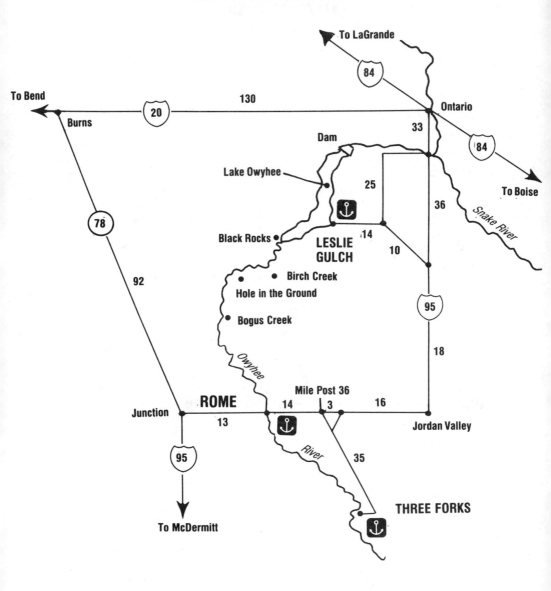

To LaGrande

84

To Bend

20 130 **Ontario**

Burns 33

84

Dam

To Boise

Lake Owyhee 25

Snake River

36

78

Black Rocks 14

LESLIE GULCH 10

92 **Birch Creek**

Hole in the Ground **95**

Bogus Creek 18

Owyhee

Mile Post 36

ROME 14 3 16

Junction 13 **Jordan Valley**

River 35

95

THREE FORKS

To McDermitt

ONE WAY SHUTTLE DISTANCE

	Miles	Hours
Rome to Three Forks	49	1:45
Rome to Leslie Gulch	75	2:30

Jordan Valley is a famous "speed trap" so beware.

Lower Owyhee River Log

Rome to Leslie Gulch

River mile: 120-65 . 55 miles plus 10 miles on reservoir
.... 65 miles
River time: 15 hours 45 minutes. 3.5 m.p.h. plus reservoir time.
Logged in raft
River slope: 14 feet per mile average
River trip discharge: 1,400 c.f.s. Rome gage
Recommended discharge: 1,000 to 4,000 c.f.s. Rome gage
River discharge information:
    National Weather Service
    (503) 261-9246
Information:
    U.S. Bureau of Land Management
    Vale District
    P. O. Box 700
    100 Oregon Street
    Vale, OR 97918
    (541) 473-3144

Shuttle information:
    Eva Easterday — vehicle shuttle, boat tow
    Jordan Valley, OR 97910
    (541) 586-2352

    Ken Haylett Enterprises — vehicle shuttle, boat tow
    P. O. Box 274
    Jordan Valley, OR 97910
    (208) 586-2406

RIVER MILE	RIVER TIME	LEFT BANK	RAPIDS	RIGHT BANK	DESCRIPTION
	4:00			⛊	
	50		• 2		
	40				Narrow canyon
	30	⛊	• 2 • 2		Upset rapid - keep left (large rock)
	20				
RM 110	10				Sand beach, right
	3:00				
	50	～～ ⛊			Canyon left
	40				
	30				Sand lunch beach left
	20			} narrow canyon	Sand lunch beach left
	10				
	2:00	～～～			Crooked Creek, left
RM 115	50				
	40				
	30				
	20				
	10				
	1:00				Elevation 3347
	50		⊏⊐	～～	Gaging station - Iron truss Jordon Creek right
	40				
RM 120	30				
	20				
	10				
	12:00		⊏⊐	⚓	Highway 95 bridge BLM launch at Rome

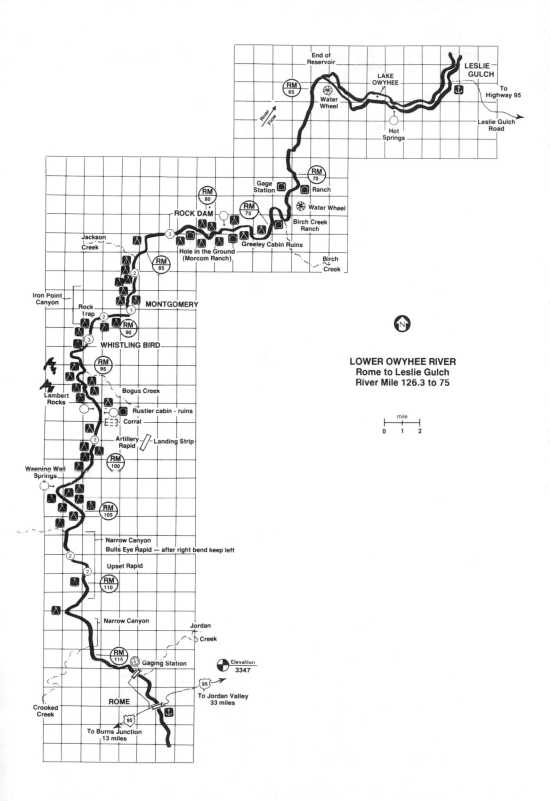

End of Reservoir

LESLIE GULCH

LAKE OWYHEE

RM 65

Water Wheel

River Flow

To Highway 95

Leslie Gulch Road

Hot Springs

RM 70

Ranch

Gage Station

Water Wheel

Birch Creek Ranch

ROCK DAM

RM 75

RM 80

Greeley Cabin Ruins

Jackson Creek

Hole in the Ground (Morcom Ranch)

Birch Creek

RM 85

Iron Point Canyon

MONTGOMERY

Rock Trap

RM 90

WHISTLING BIRD

RM 95

Bogus Creek

Lambert Rocks

Rustler cabin - ruins

Corral

Artillery Rapid

Landing Strip

RM 100

Weening Wall Springs

RM 105

Narrow Canyon

Bulls Eye Rapid — after right bend keep left

Upset Rapid

RM 110

Narrow Canyon

Jordan Creek

RM 115

Gaging Station

Elevation 3347

95

To Jordan Valley 33 miles

ROME

Crooked Creek

95

To Burns Junction 13 miles

LOWER OWYHEE RIVER
Rome to Leslie Gulch
River Mile 126.3 to 75

mile
0   1   2

199

RIVER MILE	RIVER TIME	LEFT BANK	RAPIDS	RIGHT BANK	DESCRIPTION
	8:00				
	50		2 2		Lambert Rock Area
RM 96	40				
	30				
	20				
	10		1		Fence - spring - rock shelf across river
	7:00				
	50				Rustler cabin, right
	40				Artillery rapids, scout right
RM 100	30		2		
	20		2		
	10				
	6:00				
	50		2		
	40				
	30				Weeping Wall Springs, left
	20		2		
	10				Sand beach camps, left and right
RM 105	5:00		2		
	50				
	40		2		
	30				Large side canyon, left
	20		2		
RM 108	10				Bullseye Rapid after right bend keep left
	4:00		2	canyon	

200

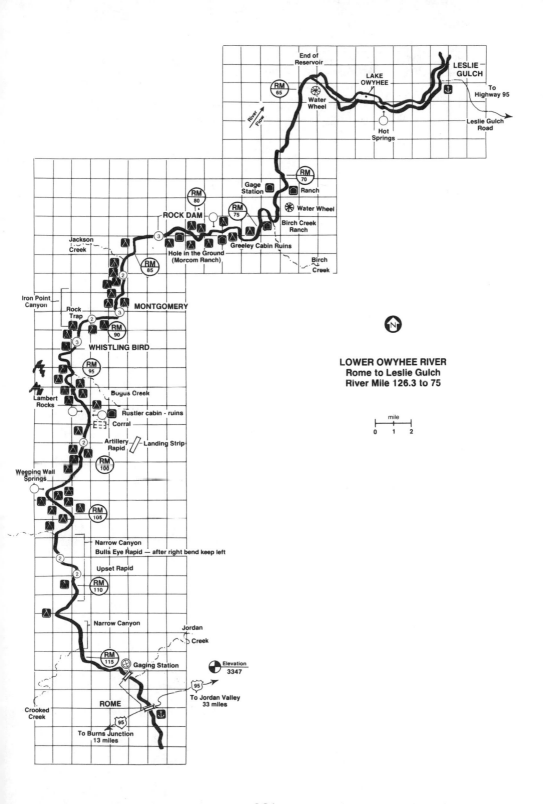

LOWER OWYHEE RIVER
Rome to Leslie Gulch
River Mile 126.3 to 75

End of Reservoir

LESLIE GULCH

LAKE OWYHEE

To Highway 95

RM 65

Water Wheel

River Flow

Hot Springs

Leslie Gulch Road

RM 70

Gage Station

Ranch

RM 80

Water Wheel

ROCK DAM

RM 75

Birch Creek Ranch

Jackson Creek

Greeley Cabin Ruins

Hole in the Ground (Morcom Ranch)

Birch Creek

RM 85

Iron Point Canyon

Rock Trap

MONTGOMERY

WHISTLING BIRD

RM 90

RM 95

Bogus Creek

Lambert Rocks

Rustler cabin - ruins

Corral

Artillery Rapid

Landing Strip

Weeping Wall Springs

RM 100

RM 105

Narrow Canyon

Bulls Eye Rapid — after right bend keep left

Upset Rapid

RM 110

Narrow Canyon

Jordan Creek

RM 115

Gaging Station

Elevation 3347

95

To Jordan Valley 33 miles

ROME

Crooked Creek

95

To Burns Junction 13 miles

mile
0 1 2

201

RIVER MILE	RIVER TIME	LEFT BANK	RAPIDS	RIGHT BANK	DESCRIPTION
	12:00			🏠	Hole In The Ground Ranch (Morcom Ranch) right
	50			⛺	
	40	～～～	• 3		Rock Dam rapids - scout right Falls high on left
RM 85	30	⛺	• 2		
	20	⊙	• 2		
	10	～⛺～			Jackson Creek left
	11:00	⛺ s L.W.	• 2		
	50				
	40	⛺ L.W.			
	30	⛺ s			
	20				
	10	⛺		⛺	Iron Point Canyon
	10:00		• 3		Montgomery rapids - scout right
RM 90	50			◯← ⛺⛺	
	40		▷ 1		
	30		2 / 2	⛺	Rock Trap rapids 5 boulders, keep right
	20	⤴ cave ⚡ ⛺	▷ 1		
	10	⛺⛺	3		Whistling Bird rapids - scout left
	9:00				
	50				
	40		2		
	30	⛺			
	20				
RM 95	10			～～～	Waterfall high on right
	8:00	～～＜			Narrow side canyon left

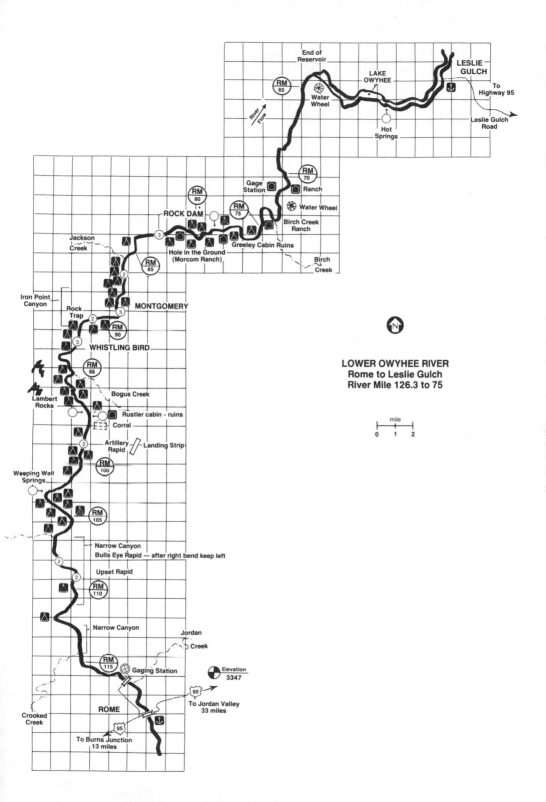

End of
Reservoir

RM
65

LAKE
OWYHEE

LESLIE
GULCH

Water
Wheel

To
Highway 95

River
Flow

Leslie Gulch
Road

Hot
Springs

Gage
Station

RM
70

Ranch

RM
80

ROCK DAM

RM
75

Water Wheel

Jackson
Creek

3

Birch Creek
Ranch

Greeley Cabin Ruins

Hole in the Ground
(Morcom Ranch)

RM
85

2

Birch
Creek

Iron Point
Canyon

Rock
Trap

3

MONTGOMERY

2

RM
90

3

WHISTLING BIRD

RM
96

Lambert
Rocks

Bogus Creek

Rustler cabin - ruins

Corral

2

Artillery
Rapid

Landing Strip

Weeping Wall
Springs

RM
100

RM
105

2

Narrow Canyon

Bulls Eye Rapid — after right bend keep left

2

Upset Rapid

2

RM
110

Narrow Canyon

Jordan

Creek

RM
115

Gaging Station

Elevation
3347

95

ROME

To Jordan Valley
33 miles

Crooked
Creek

95

To Burns Junction
13 miles

N

LOWER OWYHEE RIVER
Rome to Leslie Gulch
River Mile 126.3 to 75

mile

0   1   2

RIVER MILE	RIVER TIME	LEFT BANK	RAPIDS	RIGHT BANK	DESCRIPTION
	16:00				Ten miles to Leslie Gulch boat ramp.
	50				Start of reservior Sand Beach
	40				
RM 65	30			⊛	Water Wheel
	20	⌂			Old bridge pier right
					Old building, fences left
	10				
	15:00				
	50		⊙		Island
	40				
	30	⌂		⌂	Gage station left Ranch right
	20			⊛	Water Wheel
	10			〜〜〜	Birch Creek Ranch
RM 75	14:00			⌂	
	50		1 ⊙		Island
			1		
	40				
	30			>·〜·〜·	Narrow side canyon right
	20				
	10	▲ ▲	1	⛺	
	13:00	◯→	1	⌂	Greeley cabin ruins
	50		1		
	40	╱↗₁	1 / 2		Rock Butte high on left
	30	▲		⛺	
RM 80	20		⟩ 1		Petroglyphs left
	10	⛺		⛺	
	12:00				

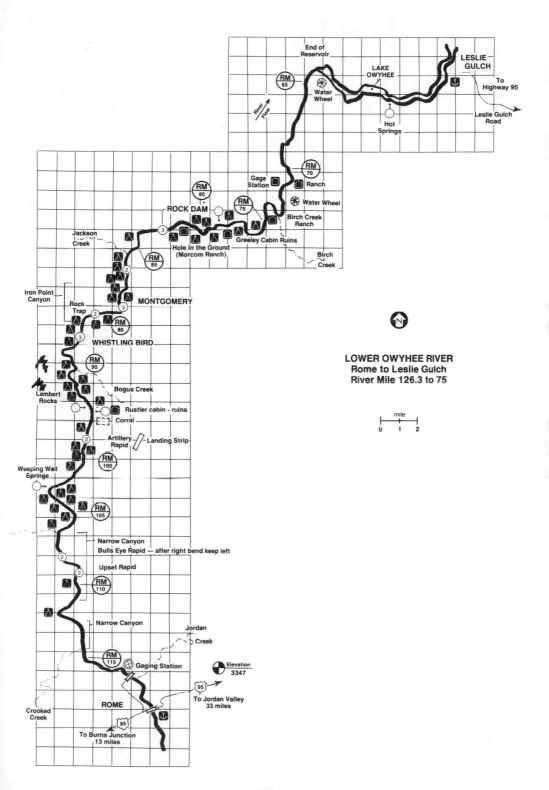

LOWER OWYHEE RIVER
Rome to Leslie Gulch
River Mile 126.3 to 75

Coffee Pot Rapids — R.M. 47

Rogue River

Graves Creek to Foster Bar

The Rogue River was a charter river in the 1968 National Wild and Scenic Rivers Act. The state followed by including 84 miles of the Rogue in the 1969 Scenic Waterways Act by initiative petition of the people. Another state initiative and the federal Omnibus Rivers bill in 1988 included an additional section of the river, giving the Rogue over 120 miles of protection. By any standard the Rogue is a river recognized nationally for its outstanding qualities.

The Rogue has its origins near Crater Lake, and it carves its way through southwestern Oregon for more than 200 miles to the Pacific Ocean. Thirty-three miles of the river are designated as "wild", and that is the section covered in this log. Actually boaters extend their trip two miles beyond the wild section to the Foster bar boat ramp for a total trip length of thirty-five miles.

The wild section of the Rogue River is so popular that it is one of three Oregon rivers with limited access during the main summer boating season and a permit to boat is required during this period. The first step to enjoying the Rogue is to get a permit, either by booking through an outfitter or through the private boater lottery system. The easiest access to the Rogue for commercial passengers is to call one of the forty outfitters and book a trip. For the private boater, the system of access is slightly different.

A lottery is held for private boaters through a private vendor. Boaters must apply December 1 through January 31, for the permit season from May 15 through October 15. The lottery vendor is Tioga Resources, Inc., P. O. Box 5149, Roseburg, OR 97470, phone (541) 672-4168 or FAX (541) 672-4192 and the application fee is $4.00. Successful applicants will pay an additional fee of $10.00 per person when confirming the permit with the Forest Service after the lottery. Administration of permits for confirmation, cancellation, no shows or dates unfilled in the lottery is by the Forest Service at the Rand Visitor Center (541) 479-3735. There are approximately 60 private boaters allowed per day during the permit season and the maximum party size is 20. The chances of obtaining a permit through the lottery varies, but is presently about one in ten. Cancellations are allocated by phone on a first come, first served basis, within nine days prior to the desired launch date.

One of the Rogue River's attractions is the whitewater. Rainie Falls, Mule Creek Canyon and Blossom Bar keep boaters in suspensful anticipation for almost the entire trip. The boater who lines Rainie Falls actually runs one class four rapids (Blossom Bar), about fourteen class three rapids and approximately 50 class two rapids. Every year

Rainie Falls Rapids — R.M. 66

Upper Black Bar Rapids — R.M. 60

Zane Grey Cabin — R.M. 53

Rogue River Ranch at Mule Creek — R.M. 48

upwards of 1,200 people boat the wild section of the Rogue along with an equal number of power boaters. It is an obviously "do-able" section of whitewater for boaters with strong class three boating skills.

Many boaters begin their trip at the Almeda Campground about three miles upstream from the beginning of the wild section at Graves Creek. The Almeda boat ramp is larger than the Graves Creek ramp which can be crowded on high use days. Immediately on leaving the boat ramp at Graves Creek, the boater enters two closely spaced class three rapids. The next rapid is Rainie Falls. This 12 foot drop is the only falls on the trip. There are three routes at Rainie Falls: the falls, a center route and the most used fish ladder adjacent to the right bank. More and more boaters are running the falls but this is a class five difficulty rapids with the attendant consequences. Rainie Falls and Blossom Bar are both crowded by picture takers. It's a temptation to run the falls when you are being recorded on film. For some unfortunate boaters the trip ends at Rainie Falls, less than one hour from the Graves Creek launch. A few of the rafters run the middle chute at Rainie Falls, but most all boaters, and particularly the drift boats, line the fish ladder. Sometimes the danger of lining on slippery rocks encourages rafters and kayakers to float and bump down the fish ladder or to portage.

Next, near river mile 64, are two closely spaced rapids called Tyee and Wildcat. Whether or not a boater scouts rapids depends primarily on his skills and his confidence in reading water. It's the boater's choice on all rapids, including Tyee and Wildcat.

From Wildcat to Black Bar are some eleven class two rapids with Russian, Howard Creek Chute, Slim Pickens and Plowshare making this section one of the more interesting on the river.

Upper Black Bar rapids at mile 60 is worth a scout. This is a popular kayak play spot. Lower Black Bar rapids is a quick class two drop followed by more class two water to Horseshoe Bend, another kayak play spot and a class three rapids. There are numerous play spots on the Rogue, including a class two "endo" rapids for kayakers near river mile 57. Actually, from Horseshoe Bend to Mule Creek is class two water with sections like the Kelsey area, a series of class two rapids, to make the trip exciting. The Zane Grey cabin, at mile 53, is in this section and is a frequent stop for boaters. The cabin is on private property, but courteous boaters are welcome.

Many boating parties attempt to camp at Mule Creek. That area fits nicely into camp schedules for the popular three day trip and is the lull before Mule Creek Canyon. The ranch at Mule Creek is on the National Historic Register and is worth the short ¼ mile hike up Mule Creek. Some boaters also hike downstream beyond Marial to look at Mule Creek Canyon.

On leaving the large eddy at Mule Creek the river begins its descent into Mule Creek Canyon. Class one rapids blend into class two, are followed by a narrow section with reflecting waves and some niches in the wall for refuge and then end at the class three Coffee Pot. Mule Creek Canyon is over a mile long and contains two class one rapids, two class two rapids and five class three rapids in close succession.

After Mule Creek Canyon is Stair Creek and The Devil's Backbone, both scenic views to the left, and then easy water to Blossom Bar. Blossom Bar rapids is intimidating at first sight because of the huge boulders which forced portage in the early days before a route was blasted through. Actually the route on the left requires only one manuever to the right and down a narrow chute followed by other rapids. The real danger is in missing the so called "cut" and going into the "picket fence". The "fence" is a series of boulders complicated by an occasional boat and numerous rescue ropes sometimes left in the river temporarily. While most boaters begin their run on the left of Blossom, some run on the right to the excitement of the large crowds that congregate at Blossom. The right bank, where boaters scout, is a popular overlook for lunch and picture taking.

Immediately after Blossom is the Devil's Staircase which is a class three rapids and a short class two, ending in an eddy at Gleason Bar camp. This is where the floater leaves a semi-wilderness area and comes into the shattering reality of 40 passenger jet boats, loud-speakers and Forest Service power boats. With poor luck on a busy day, the floater will meet some seven tour jet boats in Huggins Canyon bringing a couple hundred people into the "wild" Rogue for lunch. They will return before the floater reaches the take out, thus making, conceivably, fourteen passenger jet boaters encounters in one day on this Wild and Scenic river.

The thirty-three mile wild section of the Rogue has about 60 inventoried camps, and four of the six lodges are available for boaters booking through guides far in advance. Private boaters may some-times obtain lodging from cancellations or during the non-permit season. The rustic lodges provide accomodations that might be considered luxurious during the cold and wet "off" season.

Camps on the Rogue are not assigned, so some problems do exist, and a "lead boat race" downriver for a choice camp is not uncommon. There is a hiking trail along the river on the right bank, so camps on that side receive competition from both trail and river users. Some canyon sections have very few camps, and areas such as Horseshoe Bend, Mule Creek, Brushey Bar, Solitude and Tate Creek always seem to be popular, high use areas. There have been some problems with bears, particularly near Tate Creek. Lodge owners used to feed the bears as a tourist attraction, and the animals have now become a nuisance, ransacking campsites and sometimes damaging rafts in the process. Finding camps can be especially chaotic during the weeks after the permit season ends on October 15. At that time many boaters flock to the Rogue, often causing use to skyrocket to four or five times the 120 persons per day allowed during the permit season.

For people lucky enough to get on the Rogue it is a great experience. Special delights for the boater are exciting whitewater, salmon attempting to scale Rainie Falls, osprey folding their wings, diving to the river and then struggling skyward with a catch seemingly outweighing its captor. Deer are numerous and so tame they sometimes walk into camp for a handout. Herons, cormorants, egrets or an occasional eagle may be seen. Its fun to pretend that turkey buzzards soaring above are eagles as they wait to clean up after bears fishing for salmon. When bears tire of grubbing or chasing the wily salmon they may look for handouts at Tate Creek and that, along with the power boats in the lower section, is all part of the Rogue experience.

Tate Creek Slide — R.M. 40

Rogue River Camps

River Mile	Name	Left or Right Bank	Camp Size S, M, L,	Toilet	Comments
68.4	Grave Creek				
67.2	Sanderson Island	R	L		
66.9	Rainie — Right	R	L	●	
66.9	Rainie — Left	L	S		
66.3	China Gulch	R	S		
65.2	Whiskey Creek, Upper	R	L	●	
65.2	Whiskey Creek, Lower	R	M		
65.2	Rum Creek	L	S		
64.9	Big Slide	R	L	●	
64.9	Doe Creek	L	L	●	
64.5	Alder Creek	R	S		
64.2	Booze Creek	R	S		
63.7	Tyee — Left	L	S		
63.6	Tyee — Right	R	L	●	
63.4	Wildcat	L	L	●	Toilet Downriver
63.2	Russian	L	L		
	Montgomery Creek	L	L		
62.3	Howard Creek	L	S		
62.1	Slate Slide	R	S		
61.4	Bronco Creek	R	S		
60.4	Bunker Creek	R	L		
60.3	Big Windy Creek	L	L	●	
60.1	Black Bar Lodge				
59.7	Little Windy Creek	L	L	●	
58.9	Jenny Creek	R	L	●	
58.8	Jenny Creek	L	L		
57.7	Horseshoe Bend	R	L	●	
57.5	Horseshoe Bend, Lower	L	L		
57.4	Horseshoe Bend, Lower	R	L	●	
56.7	Meadow Creek	R	L	●	
56.5	Dulog Creek	L	L	●	

55.0	Kelsey Creek	R	L	•	
54.5	Battle Bar	L	L	•	
54.5	Ditch Creek	R	L		
53.0	Hewitt Creek	L	L	•	
52.0	Missouri Bar	L	S	•	
51.6	Quail Creek	R	L		
50.6	Long Gulch	L	L	•	
50.0	John's Rapids, Right	R	S		
50.0	John's Rapids, Left	L	S		
48.4	Mule Creek, Upper	R	L	•	
48.4	Mule Creek, Lower	R	L	•	
48.4	Mule Creek Left	L	S		
47.8	Tucker Flat (Marial)	R	L		
44.9	Gleason Bar	L	L	•	
44.5	Paradise Creek	R	S	•	
41.9	East Creek	L	S		
41.8	Brushey Bar	R	L	•	
41.5	Brushey Bar Creek	R	S	•	
41.3	Solitude Bar, Upper	R	L		
41.1	Solitude Bar, Middle	R	L	•	
40.9	Solitude Bar, Lower	R	L	•	
39.7	Tate Creek	R	L	•	Tate Creek "Slide"
39.4	Tate Creek, Lower	R	L	•	
39.2	Tacoma	R	L	•	
39.1	Tacoma, Lower	R	S		
37.3	Flora Dell	R	L	•	
36.5	Hicks Creek	R	L		
35.5	Watson Creek				
33.8	Foster Creek				
33.5	Foster Bar				

ROGUE RIVER

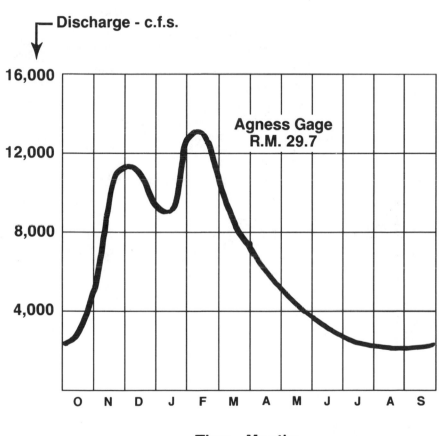

Discharge - c.f.s.

Agness Gage
R.M. 29.7

16,000

12,000

8,000

4,000

O N D J F M A M J J A S

Time - Months

SHUTTLE MAP
Rogue and Illinois Rivers

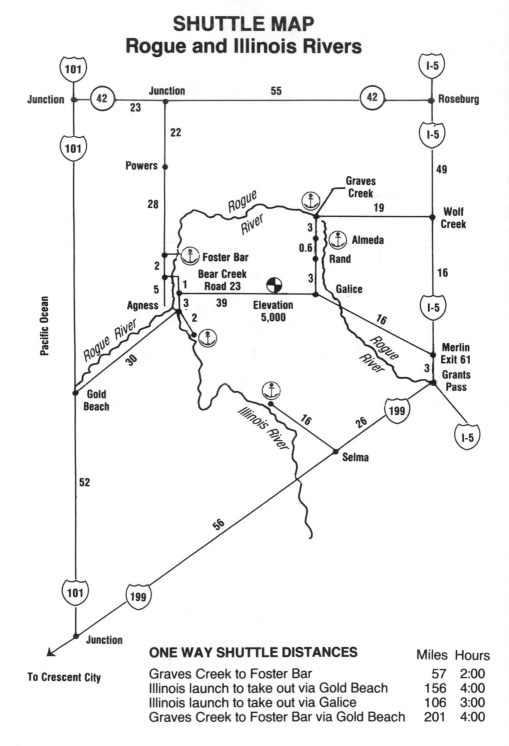

Junction

101

42 Junction 55 42 Roseburg

I-5

101 23

22 I-5

Powers 49

28 Rogue River Graves Creek 19 Wolf Creek

Foster Bar 3 Almeda

0.6 Rand

Bear Creek Road 23 2

5 1 3 Galice

Agness 3 39 Elevation 5,000 16

2 Rogue River

Rogue River

30 Merlin Exit 61
3 Grants Pass

16

Gold Beach

Illinois River 16 26 199

Selma I-5

52

56

101 199

Junction

To Crescent City

I-5

Pacific Ocean

16

ONE WAY SHUTTLE DISTANCES

	Miles	Hours
Graves Creek to Foster Bar	57	2:00
Illinois launch to take out via Gold Beach	156	4:00
Illinois launch to take out via Galice	106	3:00
Graves Creek to Foster Bar via Gold Beach	201	4:00

Rogue River Log

Graves Creek to Foster Bar

River mile: 68 to 33 .... 35 miles
Drift time: 11 hours 30 minutes .... 3 m.p.h.
Logged in raft
River slope: 13 feet per mile average
River discharge: 2,000 c.f.s. Agness gage
Recommended discharge; 1,000 to 4,000 c.f.s.
River discharge information:
    National Weather Service   (503) 261-9246
Information:
    Managed jointly by:
    Bureau of Land Management
    Medford, Oregon
        and
    U.S. Forest Service
    Grants Pass, Oregon
Private boater lottery permit applications: December 1 through January 31.
    Tioga Resources, Inc. (541) 672-4168
    Permit season, May 15 through October 15
Information after the lottery:
    Permit confirmation, cancellations, no shows, unfilled dates.
    U. S. Forest Service
    Rand Information Center
    14335 Galice Road
    Merlin, Oregon 97532
    (541) 479-3735
Car shuttle:
    Galice Resort (541) 476-3818
    Both the Bear Springs road and Powers route may be closed.
    Shuttles must them be done via Gold Beach.
Lodges:
    Morrison's Lodge (R.M.78), (541) 476-3825, 1-800-826-1963
    Black Bar Lodge (R.M. 60) 541-479-6507
    Marial Lodge (R.M. 47), (541) 474-2057
      Mobile Net (541) 479-4923 Ask for 7718
    Paradise Lodge (R.M. 44) (541) 247-6022
                    247-6504
    Half Moon Bar Lodge (R.M. 44), (541) 247-6968
    Clay Hill Lodge (R.M. 39), (541) 247-6215
    Wild River Lodge (R.M. 36), (541) 247-6215

    Rogue River Reservations, Inc.
    Bookings for above lodges
    Toll Free 1-800-525-2161

RIVER MILE	RIVER TIME	LEFT BANK	RAPIDS	RIGHT BANK	DESCRIPTION
	4:00			🛶	
	50		• 2 • 2	〰	Meadow Creek
•	40	⛺	• 2 • 2	🛶 ⛺	HORSHOE BEND RAPIDS
	30		• 3 ▷ 2	🛶	
•	20	〰 ⛺			Jenny Creek
	10				
•	3:00	〰 🛶			Little Windy Creek
	50	⛺			Black Bar Lodge
RM 60	40	〰 ⛺	• 2 • 3		UPPER BLACK BAR RAPIDS scout right Big Windy Creek left
	30		▷ 2	〰 ⛺	Windy Creek Rapids
•	20		▷ 2		Plowshare Rapids Washboard Rapids
	10				
•	2:00	⛺	• 2	⛺ ⛺	Slim Pickens Rapids Howard Creek
•	50	〰	•		
	40		▷ 2		
	30	⛺		〰	Russian Creek
•	20	⛺	• 3		WILDCAT RAPIDS
	10	⛺	• 3	⛺ ⛺ ⛺	TYEE RAPIDS
RM 65	1:00	⛺		⛺	
	50	〰 ⛺		〰 ⛺	Rum Creek left Whiskey Creek right
•	40			⛺	
	30	⛺	• 5	⛺	RAINIE FALLS line or run right Fish ladder route
•	20				
	10			⛺	Graves Creek Falls
•	12:00		3 • • 3	⚓	Graves Creek Rapids Graves Creek Launch
			⎵		Graves Creek Bridge

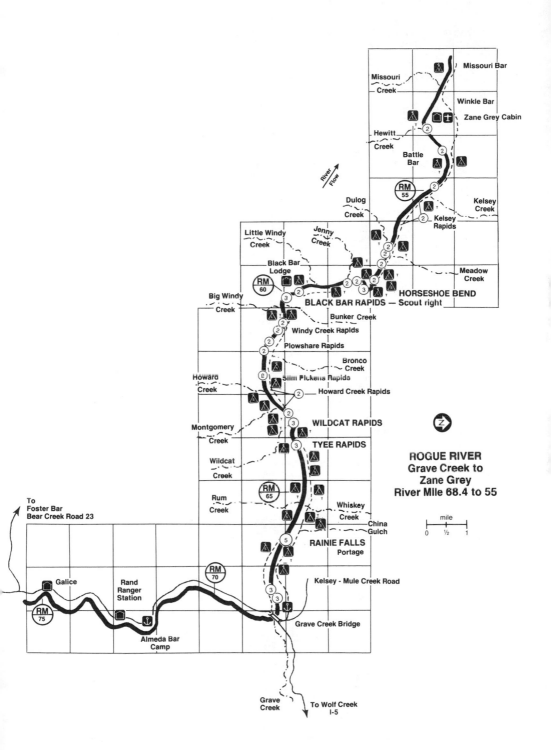

Missouri Bar

Missouri
Creek

Winkle Bar

Zane Grey Cabin

Hewitt
Creek

Battle Bar

RM 55

Dulog
Creek

Kelsey
Creek

Jenny
Creek

Kelsey
Rapids

Little Windy
Creek

Meadow
Creek

Black Bar
Lodge

RM 60

HORSESHOE BEND

Big Windy
Creek

BLACK BAR RAPIDS — Scout right

Bunker Creek

Windy Creek Rapids

Plowshare Rapids

Bronco
Creek

Howard
Creek

Slim Pickens Rapids

Howard Creek Rapids

Montgomery
Creek

WILDCAT RAPIDS

TYEE RAPIDS

Wildcat
Creek

RM 65

Rum
Creek

Whiskey
Creek

China
Gulch

To
Foster Bar
Bear Creek Road 23

RAINIE FALLS

Portage

River
Flow

Z

ROGUE RIVER
Grave Creek to
Zane Grey
River Mile 68.4 to 55

mile

0   ½   1

Galice

Rand
Ranger
Station

RM 70

Kelsey - Mule Creek Road

RM 75

Almeda Bar
Camp

Grave Creek Bridge

Grave
Creek

To Wolf Creek
I-5

219

RIVER MILE	RIVER TIME	LEFT BANK	RAPIDS	RIGHT BANK	DESCRIPTION
	8:00				
	50		2	🏠 ✝	Paradise Lodge, airstrip
	40		2 3		
RM 45	30	⛺T	3 4	⛺T	DEVILS STAIRCASE RAPIDS
	20				BLOSSOM BAR RAPIDS — scout right
	10				Devils Backbone high on left
	7:00				Stair Creek left COFFEE POT RAPIDs
	50		3		Mule Creek Canyon
	40		2	🏠	Marial Lodge
	30	⛺S		⛺	
	20		2	⛺🏠	Mule Creek Ranch
RM 50	10		2		China Bar Rapids
	6:00	⛺S	2 2	⛺S	Maggie's Rapids John's Rapids
	50		2 2		
	40	⛺T	2		Long Gulch Creek
	30	⛺S		⛺	Quail Creek right Missouri Creek left
	20				
	10				
	5:00	⛺T		🏠 ✝	Zane Grey cabin, airstrip Hewitt Creek
	50		2		
	40	⛺T	2		
	30				Battle Bar
RM 55	20			⛺T	Kelsey Creek
	10				Kelsey Rapids
	4:00	⛺T	2		

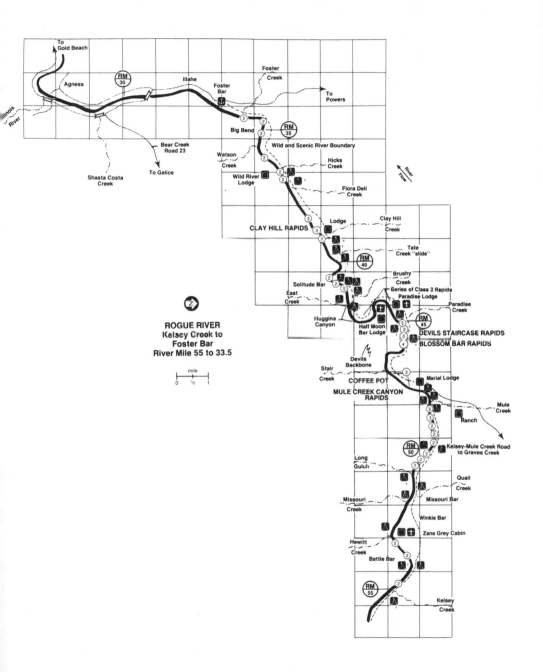

To
Gold Beach

Agness

Illahe

Foster
Creek

Foster
Bar

To
Powers

RM
30

Illinois
River

Bear Creek
Road 23

To Galice

Shasta Costa
Creek

Big Bend

RM
35

Wild and Scenic River Boundary

Watson
Creek

Hicks
Creek

Wild River
Lodge

Flora Dell
Creek

CLAY HILL RAPIDS

Lodge

Clay Hill
Creek

Tate
Creek "slide"

RM
40

Brushy
Creek

Solitude Bar

Series of Class 2 Rapids

East
Creek

Paradise Lodge

Paradise
Creek

Huggins
Canyon

Half Moon
Bar Lodge

RM
45

DEVILS STAIRCASE RAPIDS

BLOSSOM BAR RAPIDS

Stair
Creek

Devils
Backbone

Marial Lodge

COFFEE POT

MULE CREEK CANYON
RAPIDS

Mule
Creek

Ranch

ROGUE RIVER
Kelsey Creek to
Foster Bar
River Mile 55 to 33.5

RM
50

Kelsey-Mule Creek Road
to Graves Creek

mile
0   ½   1

Long
Gulch

Quail
Creek

Missouri
Creek

Missouri Bar

Winkle Bar

Zane Grey Cabin

Hewitt
Creek

Battle Bar

RM
55

Kelsey
Creek

221

RIVER MILE	RIVER TIME	LEFT BANK	RAPIDS	RIGHT BANK	DESCRIPTION
	12:00				
	50				
	40				
	30			⚓	Foster Bar boat ramp
	20		1		
RM 35	10		1		Illahe riffle
	11:00	⛺	2		Big bend area
	50				Watson Creek Wild River boundary
	40	⛺	2		
	30	🏠	2		Wild River lodge
			2		
	20				
	10			⛺ T	
					Flora Dell Creek
	10:00				
	50				
	40		2 3	🏠	CLAY HILL RAPIDS Clay Hill lodge
	30		2	🏠	Clay Hill Creek
RM 40	20			⛺ T ⛺ T	Tate Creek "Slide"
	10			⛺ T	
	9:00			⛺ ⛺ T	Solitude Bar camps
	50		}2	⛺	
	40	⛺ M		⛺ S	
	30	~~~ ~~~		⛺ T	East Creek Brushy Bar area
	20				Huggins Canyon
	10				
	8:00	🏠 ✚	}2		Half Moon Bar lodge, Airstrip

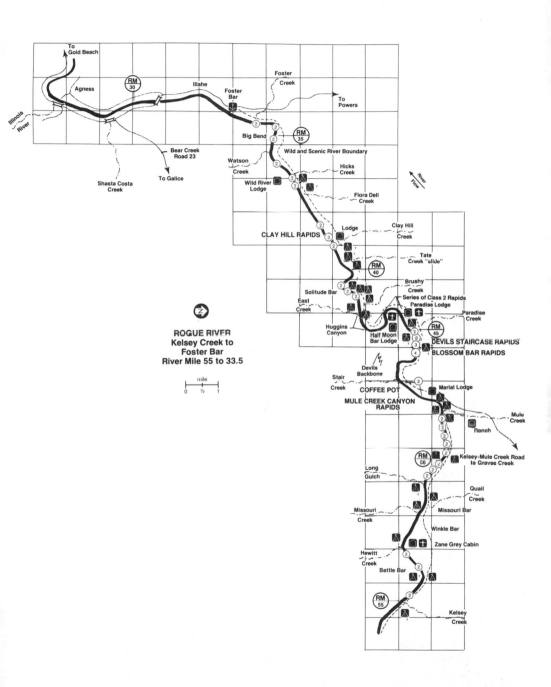

To
Gold Beach

Agness

Illinois
River

RM
30

Illahe

Foster
Bar

Foster
Creek

To Powers

2
2
Big Bend
2

RM
35

Wild and Scenic River Boundary

Bear Creek
Road 23

Watson
Creek

2

Hicks
Creek

Wild River
Lodge

Shasta Costa
Creek

To Galice

Flora Dell
Creek

2

Lodge

Clay Hill
Creek

CLAY HILL RAPIDS

3

Tate
Creek "slide"

RM
40

Brushy
Creek

ROGUE RIVER
Kelsey Creek to
Foster Bar
River Mile 55 to 33.5

mile
0   ½   1

Solitude Bar

East
Creek

2

Series of Class 2 Rapids
Paradise Lodge

Paradise
Creek

RM
45

Huggins
Canyon

Half Moon
Bar Lodge

3

DEVILS STAIRCASE RAPIDS

BLOSSOM BAR RAPIDS

Devils
Backbone

Stair
Creek

3

Marial Lodge

COFFEE POT

MULE CREEK CANYON
RAPIDS

Mule
Creek

2

Ranch

2

Kelsey-Mule Creek Road
to Graves Creek

RM
50

2

Long
Gulch

2

Quail
Creek

Missouri
Creek

Missouri Bar

Winkle Bar

Zane Grey Cabin

Hewitt
Creek

Battle Bar

2

RM
55

2

Kelsey
Creek

River
Flow

Mule Creek Canyon — Devils Backbone

Blossom Bar Rapids — R.M. 45

Blossom Bar Rapids — R.M. 45

Pipeline Rapids — R.M. 18

Sandy River

Dodge Park to Dabney Park

The Sandy River is included in the State Scenic Waterways System and in the Federal Wild and Scenic Rivers Act. The river is close to over a million people in the greater Portland metropolitan area, and it serves as a convenient day trip for local boaters. During the fall, winter and spring high water months, when the weather is often cold and rainy, the Sandy River is popular with steelhead fishermen and boaters. During the summer when most of the fishermen and boaters are elsewhere, the river is besieged with recreationists who are less concerned with minimum water flows. Good weather fills Lewis and Clark, Dabney, Oxbow and Dodge Parks to overflowing.

The Sandy River has its origins at Reid Glacier on Mount Hood. It flows over 55 miles westerly to the Columbia River at Troutdale. The river has been boated from McNeil Campground near river mile 50 to the mouth. The upper sections are small flow, usually must be boated at flood stage and are not recommended for the casual boater. The Sandy Gorge from Marmot Diversion Dam (R.M. 30) to Revenue Bridge (R.M. 24) near Sandy is a short section of class four to five water at almost any stage, and it should be run only in the company of someone familiar with the section. Most Sandy River floaters boat from Dodge Park (R.M. 19) to any of the parks downstream. Beginning boaters prefer the shortest and easiest section of the Sandy from Oxbow Park (R.M. 11) downstream to Dabney or Lewis and Clark Parks. There is a gaging station near Dodge Park just below the confluence of the Bull Run River, and the gage readings are available from the National Weather Service. This log is for Dodge Park to Dabney Park.

The boater launching from Dodge Park is immediately into a class two rapids which becomes class three at some river stages. It is a good idea to hike down the left bank from Dodge Park to Pipeline Bridge and look at Pipeline Rapids, probably the most difficult rapids on the trip. Just beyond this rapids is a high cliff with a sharp left turn. High Cliff is a series of three closely spaced class two rapids on the left turn. Just beyond High Cliff Rapids is the Blue Hole, a long class two rapids ending at a right bend in the river and a sandy beach. After Blue Hole is a left turn then a right turn with two channels at high water. On these two turns are three closely spaced class two rapids. All of these rapids occur within the first three miles of the trip and within approximately one half hour depending on the river flow. The rapids downstream from Indian John Island, river mile 15, are routine, not exceeding class two, and are not shown on the map. The first boater exit is at the Oxbow Park launch, followed by the launches downstream at Dabney and at Lewis and Clark Parks. The river section from Dodge Park to Oxbow Park is in a deep forested and isolated gorge containing the best scenery and whitewater on the trip.

Sandy River Log

Dodge Park to Dabney Park

River mile: 15.8 to 15.9 .... 13 miles
Logged in canoe
Drift time: 2 hours 45 minutes .... 4.5 m.p.h.
River slope: 13 feet per mile average
River discharge: 1,700 c.f.s.
Recommended discharge: 1,500 to 4,000 c.f.s.
River discharge information:
    National Weather Service
    (503) 261-9246

SANDY RIVER

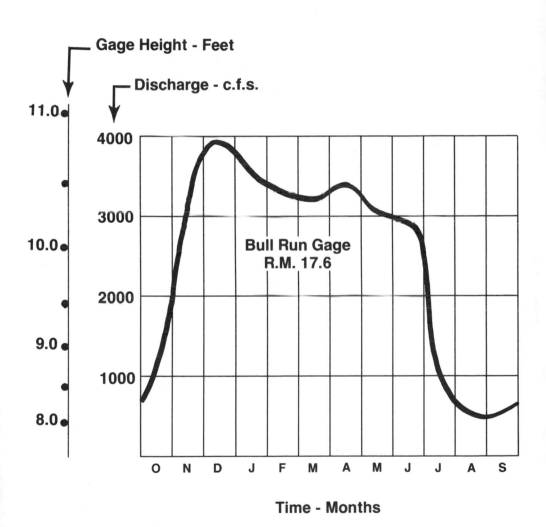

Gage Height - Feet

Discharge - c.f.s.

Bull Run Gage
R.M. 17.6

Time - Months

229

RIVER MILE	RIVER TIME	LEFT BANK	RAPIDS	RIGHT BANK	DESCRIPTION
RM 6					
	3:00				
	50			⚓	Dabney State Park
	40		⊙		
	30		⊙ ⊙		Islands
RM 10	20		⊙	〜〜〜	Big Creek
	10				
	2:00				
	50	⚓			Oxbow Park boat ramp
	40		⊙	〜〜〜	Gordon Creek
	30				
	20		⊙ ⊙		Islands
RM 15	10	⌂	2 1 ⊙		Indian John Island
	1:00		2 ⊙ ⊙		
	50		2 ⊙		Islands
	40		2 ⊙ 2		
	30		2		Blue Hole - Sandy beach / Long rapids
	20		2		
	10		2 2		High Cliff area
	12:00		3 • 2	〜〜〜	PIPELINE RAPIDS / Bull Run River
RM 19				⚓	Launch - Dodge Park

230

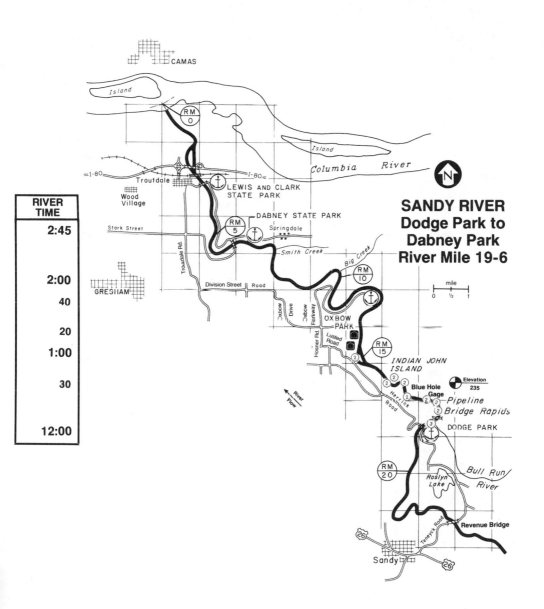

SANDY RIVER
Dodge Park to
Dabney Park
River Mile 19-6

North Santiam River

Packsaddle Park to Mehama

A river convenient to many Oregonians, and one that provides challenging boating sections, is the North Santiam. McKenzie-type drift boats, canoe, kayaks and rubber rafts run this river regularly. For an open canoe there are several rapids that at certain stages are most challenging.

The upper section of the river above the backwaters of Detroit Dam parallels the road for long stretches. We looked at this section, then decided it was too difficult for an open-canoe trip. The section below Big Cliff regulating dam, at river mile 48.1 to Packsaddle Park at river mile 54.5, is dangerous for any boat. (Niagara Park in this section is appropriately named.) Our trip took us from Packsaddle Park at river mile 54.4 to river mile 38.7 at the Mehama Bridge.

Before starting this trip, stop at the bridge in Mill City and look at the rapids under the bridge. This will let you decide whether you want to run straight through, or get out just before the rapids. The next rapids to scout before starting the trip is Spencers Hole. To view Spencers Hole, turn west or downstream on Central Street in the town of Gates for 0.7 mile to a wooded trail to the river. Here you can see both Spencers Hole and the rapids preceding it. Both are less than 17 minutes by boat downstream from the Gates bridge.

This log is for discharge of 2,500 c.f.s. at the Big Cliff Regulating Dam. This is a desirable stage to run the river. It is high enough to cover many shallow or rocky sections and still provide small rapid sections to make the trip interesting.

In the very beginning of the trip, as you start from Packsaddle Park, which is the start of what is locally called the "Whitewater Challenge", there are continuous minor rapids. We recorded 13 of these rapids before Spencers Hole and all within one hour river time. Almost half the rapids on this trip occur within the first hour river time. There are actually only four major rapids on the entire trip. In one of these rapids we swamped an open canoe. The cause was a boating error rather than the complexity of the rapids. This error also reminded us how cold the North Santiam usually is. Many boaters wear wet suits on this river, particularly in the early part of the season.

Of all the rapids on the North Santiam we scout only the two mentioned and run all of them. If you can handle Spencers Hole and Mill City Bridge Rapids, you should be able to successfully negotiate the others.

Just before Mill City Bridge Rapids there is a sharp right bend in the river. Around this bend is a class two rapids that becomes difficult, particularly at lower river stages. Immediately after this rapids pull into an eddy on the right as soon as you can see the Mill City Bridge. This is a convenient place to get out. If you pass this point, there is a high wall on the right which might force the boater over the Mill City Bridge Rapids, whether he wants to boat them or not. Frequently boaters who did not scout these rapids before starting the trip, land on the left bank to scout. Mill City Bridge Rapids is run regularly by boaters in all types of craft.

Many boaters stop their trip at Fisherman Bend Park shortly downstream from Mill City. It is easy to miss this camp, and the unimproved boat landing is obscured by bank brush. If you miss this park, the next exit is another park about 45 minutes downstream. There are interesting rapids all the way below Fisherman Bend to the Mehama boat ramp. The convenient trip exit locations are at Mill City, Fisherman Bend Park, the park at river mile 43.7 and the boat ramp at Mehama. From Mehama to Stayton is a leisurely trip with only two points to watch, the sharp rock shelf just after the first transmission line crossing of the river and the fish ladder falls portage. We have taken the right channel at this portage in an attempt to find a passage without portage. Invariably as you pass through or by the maze of channels, interconnecting channels, headgates and other fish ladders or small dams, you end up in a power canal having to portage at least once anyway. Most boaters do not go downstream from Mehama. If you do go downstream from Mehama, stay in the left channel at the first main dam and fish ladder (river mile 31.3). Small boats can portage on the left bank near the ladder, and drift boats can, with some difficulty, portage over the 6 foot falls by landing on the point of the island. Portage at the fish ladder has the added advantage of being able to observe the salmon during the migrating season. River exit is at the Stayton Bridge.

North Santiam River Log

Packsaddle Park to Mehama

River mile: 54.4 to 38.7 .... 16 miles
Drift time: 3 hours 40 minutes .... 4.2 m.p.h.
Logged in raft
River slope: 23 feet per mile average
River discharge: 2,500 c.f.s. Big Cliff Dam gage
Recommended discharge: 1,500 to 4,000 c.f.s.
River discharge information:
    National Weather Service
    (503) 261-9246

NORTH SANTIAM RIVER

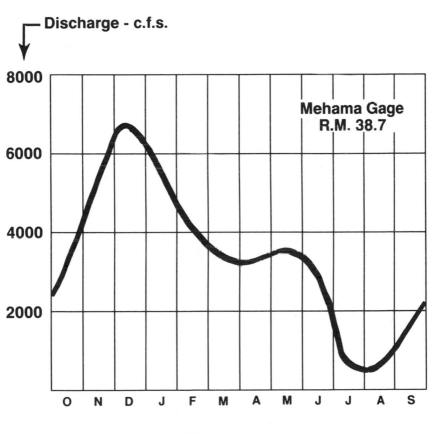

Discharge - c.f.s.

Mehama Gage
R.M. 38.7

Time - Months

RIVER MILE	RIVER TIME	LEFT BANK	RAPIDS	RIGHT BANK	DESCRIPTION
	2:00				
	55				
RM 45	50				
	45				
	40				
	35		3 • (bridge)		MILL CITY BRIDGE — SCOUT RAPIDS
	30		2 •		Warning for Mill City Rapids Concrete wall right
	25				
	20				
	15	〰〰			
	10	〰〰	1 • / 1 • / 1 • / 2 •		
	05				
	1:00				
	55		3 • / 2 •		SPENCERS HOLE — Scout
RM 50	50		1 • / 1 •		
	45		1 • / 1 • / 1 •		
	40		(bridge)		Gates Bridge
	35				
	30		1 •		
	25				
	20		1 • / 1 •		
	15				
	10		2 • / 1 •		
	05		2 • / 1 •		
RM 55	12:00		1 •	⚓	Packsaddle Park

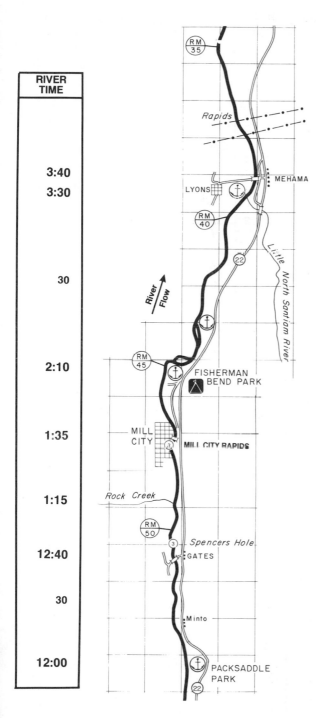

RIVER TIME	
3:40	
3:30	
30	
2:10	
1:35	
1:15	
12:40	
30	
12:00	

RM 35

Rapids

MEHAMA

LYONS

RM 40

Little North Santiam River

22

River Flow

RM 45

FISHERMAN BEND PARK

MILL CITY

MILL CITY RAPIDS

Rock Creek

RM 50

3 *Spencers Hole*

GATES

Minto

PACKSADDLE PARK

22

NORTH SANTIAM RIVER
Packsaddle Park to Mehama

mile

0   ½   1

237

RIVER MILE	RIVER TIME	LEFT BANK	RAPIDS	RIGHT BANK	DESCRIPTION
	4:00				
	55				
	50		1		
	45				Concrete bridge pier right
	40		1		
	35	⚓	� (bridge)		Mehama Bridge
	30		1 ⊙	〰	Little North Santiam River
	25	⌂	⊙		
RM 40	20		1		
	15		1		
	10				
	05		⊙		
	3:00		⊙		
	55		2		
	50			⌂	
	45				
	40				
	35		2 2		
	30		2 2		
	25				
RM 45	20		⊙ 1 ⊙		
	15		1		
	10		2	🏕	Rapids after right bend Fisherman Bend Camp
	05		⊙		
	2:00				

238

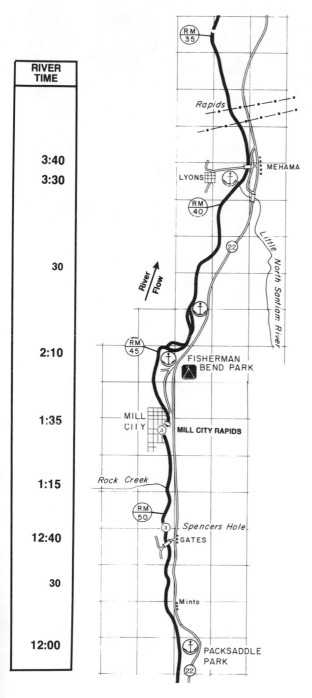

RIVER TIME	
3:40	MEHAMA
3:30	LYONS
	RM 40
	22
30	
2:10	RM 45 — FISHERMAN BEND PARK
1:35	MILL CITY — MILL CITY RAPIDS
1:15	Rock Creek
	RM 50
12:40	Spencers Hole — GATES
30	Minto
12:00	PACKSADDLE PARK

Rapids

River Flow

Little North Santiam River

NORTH SANTIAM RIVER
Packsaddle Park to Mehama

mile
0   ½   1

South Santiam River

Foster Dam to Waterloo Park

A convenient day trip in the central Willamette Valley is the South Santiam River. The section from just below Foster Dam to the park just before Waterloo Falls lends itself to intermediate boating skills because there are no rapids exceeding class two difficulty. The trip begins at the boat ramp at Foster Dam in the park on the left bank and ends at the Waterloo Park just before Waterloo Falls. Before beginning the trip, look at Waterloo Falls to assure being oriented to the proper take out location.

There are short boating sections above Foster Dam that require expert boating skills, preferably in company with a boater who has run these sections before.

Foster Dam regulates river discharge, and during the summer flows will be about 600 to 1,000 c.f.s. This South Santiam trip can be an easy, laid back drift through farmland, and the boater will hardly notice going through Sweet Home, the one town on the trip. Fishermen enjoy this section of the river, competing for fish with osprey, herons and ducks. The South Santiam is typical of many Oregon rivers that provide easy day trips for the intermediate boater.

South Santiam River Log

Foster Dam to Waterloo Park

River mile: 37.7 to 23.4 .... 14 miles
Drift time: 3 hours 40 minutes .... 4 m.p.h.
Logged in canoe
River slope: 11 feet per mile average
River discharge: 800 c.f.s. Waterloo gage
Recommended discharge: 1,000 to 3,000 c.f.s.
River discharge information:
    National Weather Service
    (503) 261-9246

SOUTH SANTIAM RIVER

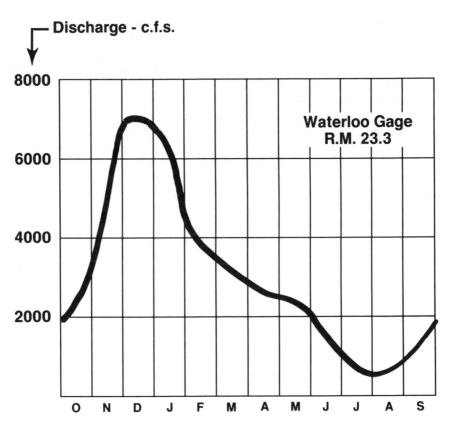

Discharge - c.f.s.

8000

6000

4000

2000

Waterloo Gage
R.M. 23.3

O N D J F M A M J J A S

Time - Months

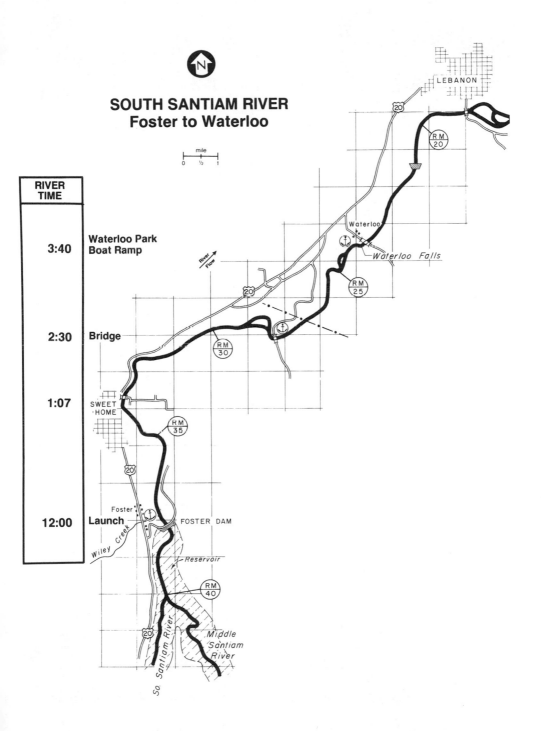

SOUTH SANTIAM RIVER
Foster to Waterloo

N

mile
0   ½   1

LEBANON

20

RM
20

Waterloo

Waterloo Falls

River Flow

RM
25

20

RIVER	TIME

3:40 — Waterloo Park Boat Ramp

2:30 — Bridge

RM
30

1:07 — SWEET HOME

RM
35

20

12:00 — Launch — Foster — FOSTER DAM

Wiley Creek

Reservoir

RM
40

20

So Santiam River

Middle Santiam River

Granite Falls Rapids — R.M. 239

Wild Sheep Creek Rapids — R.M. 241

Hells Canyon of the Snake River

Hells Canyon Dam to Grande Ronde River

The Snake River originates just north of Jackson Lake, Wyoming near the Yellowstone Park southern boundary. From Wyoming the river carves its way through southern Idaho, providing power and irrigation in an agricultural area that would otherwise be desert. The duties of the Snake were clearly defined many years ago. After making Southern Idaho bloom from irrigation, it would provide an entire series of dams through the non-agricultural Hells Canyon. These dams were planned in a manner that would make the Snake a contiguous group of lakes, linking dam forebay to dam tailrace and harnessing this river in what was just one resource in an entire development plan for the Columbia River Basin. The Snake River is over 1,000 miles long, winding through four states and draining an area larger than the state of Idaho. Anyone could see its potential energy and importance to the West.

It became a matter of not whether to develop this resource, but how. Engineers and politicians wrangled for years over such technical problems as High Sheep Dam vs. Low Sheep Dam. While this controversy was taking place in the design rooms, political arenas and courts, the public mood was changing to a course of action no one had originally considered seriously — the no-build option. Americans can credit former Justice William O. Douglas with his famous decision that was instrumental in paving the way for no more dams within Hells Canyon. In essence, Justice Douglas ordered the Federal Power Commission to rehear the entire case with adequate consideration to be given to the question of whether or not there should be any dam at all. That isn't what the power company litigants in the Supreme Court decision had in mind. The National Wild and Scenic Rivers Act of 1968 was the forerunner of later acts that would protect Hells Canyon in its free flowing natural state. In 1975 the National Recreation Act was signed into law, and a 31-mile section of the Snake River, between Hells Canyon Dam and Pittsburg Landing, became a wild section of the National Wild and Scenic River System. The 36-mile section from River Mile 180.1 to Pittsburg Landing has been designated a Scenic River.

To many boaters, the most outstanding section is the first 17 miles from Hells Canyon to Johnsons Bar. This is the most interesting from any view, scenery, wilderness or rapids. By measuring from the top of 9,400 foot Seven Devils Mountains on the Idaho side or rugged peaks on the Oregon side, you come up with the fact that this is the deepest canyon on the North American continent. Hells Canyon is majestic by any standard, whether it be looking up from the river or a mile down from Hat Point on the Oregon side.

Starting your trip from the Hells Canyon Dam boat launch, you go only five miles downstream before you come to the first class five rapids on the tour — Wild Sheep Creek Rapids. We always scout this rapids and have run it on the left (Oregon tongue), the center and the right (Idaho side). It depends mainly on your skill, equipment and attitude where to run it, so scout and decide. I have run Wild Sheep in the small rafts, affectionately called "The Yellow Peril", and friends of mine have run it in open canoes.

The next, and only other, class five rapids is Granite Falls. We always scout on the left and usually run on the left, or Oregon side, although there is a route on the Idaho side also. Again, members of our party have run it left, right and down the center. Anyone who runs this rapids down the center, excepting possibly the large commercial rafts, is asking for trouble. I never intended to run the center into the huge hole; it was just an error and something never forgotten. Granite has my attention and respect. At most river stages it is a lot of whitewater in a short distance. Although Wild Sheep and Granite are class five rapids, they could both be portaged fairly easily by kayakers, but rafts would have a difficult time, which is probably the reason most boaters run both these rapids after scouting.

There are three class three rapids at Bernard Creek that provide excitement, yet we do not scout them. We do scout Waterspout and Rush Creek when new boaters are along. Waterspout is deceptive because there is a large rock left of center near the end of the rapids that can flip most any raft. The deception is the current which actually draws boaters into this hazard, and I suspect the number of boaters "flipping" in Waterspout approaches the number for Wild Sheep Creek Rapids. It is apparent which route to take at Rush Creek if you scout, or at least can read water reasonably well.

The upper section from Hells Canyon Dam to Johnsons Bar is my favorite part of the river. That is where the rapids, wildlife and scenery are, and by comparison to the lower sections, it is more of a wilderness experience. Actually, power boats run the full length of the river. As a practical matter, the power tourist boats run downstream from the Dam to Wild Sheep Creek Rapids. Other power boats run unrestricted upstream to Granite Creek. These two rapids form a natural barrier to most power boats, leaving less than two miles between them free of power boats in this wild section.

Most of the camps in the upper section are on benches above the river. The shoreline is rocky with few sandy beaches and sometimes difficult landings. Dam discharges may fluctuate widely, requiring that boats be tied at a high elevation. We have been on the river when discharge varied between 5,000-20,000 c.f.s. in one day. This can easily be a river elevation change of four feet and can significantly change some rapids. In climbing to high elevation camps, watch for poison ivy; it is all over. In August it is usually a temptation to sleep in the dry, open starlight, but we recently have adopted the practice of sleeping only in tents. We were startled one night by a rattlesnake only an arm's length from our open bed.

Boaters on the Snake compete for camps with other river corridor users including hikers, horse packers, and power boaters. The potential for camp conflicts exist, particularly below Granite Creek and Johnsons Bar. It is best to have alternate camps in mind.

The first exit point from the river is Pittsburg Landing on the Idaho side. The next exit is Dug Bar downstream on the Oregon side. The shuttle into Dug Bar is through outstanding scenery, but is difficult so that few people exit there. The majority of people terminate their trip at Hellers Bar near the mouth of the Grande Ronde River. Pittsburg Landing is the terminus of the Wild River section and is convenient as an exit for Idaho people and for those combining Hells Canyon with the Lower Salmon trip. An increasing number of private boaters exit at Pittsburg to avoid the power boats with their camp conflicts, and because the remainder of the trip to Hellers Bar is noted for its upriver wind and lack of whitewater. Should you combine this tour with a Lower Salmon River trip, you will experience the last 20 miles of the trip on the Snake from the confluence of the Salmon to Hellers Bar near the mouth of the Grande Ronde River.

Snake River Canyon — R.M. 246

SNAKE RIVER

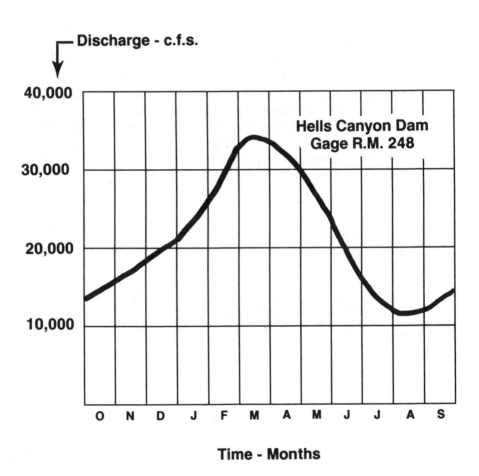

Discharge - c.f.s.

Hells Canyon Dam
Gage R.M. 248

Time - Months

SHUTTLE MAP
GRANDE RONDE - SNAKE RIVERS

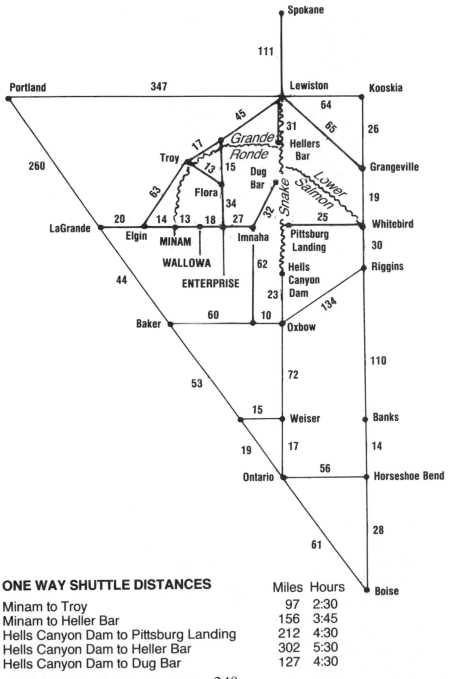

ONE WAY SHUTTLE DISTANCES

	Miles	Hours
Minam to Troy	97	2:30
Minam to Heller Bar	156	3:45
Hells Canyon Dam to Pittsburg Landing	212	4:30
Hells Canyon Dam to Heller Bar	302	5:30
Hells Canyon Dam to Dug Bar	127	4:30

249

Hells Canyon of the Snake River Campsites

River Mile	Name	Left or Right Bank	Camp Size	Toilet	Good Landing	Shade
245.8	Lamont Springs	R	30		x	
245.2	Square Beach	R	10		x	
244.7	Brush Creek	R	15		x	
243.8	Rocky Point	R	15		x	x
243.4	Chimney Bar	R	30			x
243.2	Warm Springs	R	30	T		x
242.1	Battle Creek	L	30	T	x	x
241.8	Sand Dunes	L	10		x	
241.6	Birch Springs	R	15			
241.4	Wild Sheep	L	30	T		
240.8	Rocky Bar	R	30			x
239.7	Upper Granite Creek	R	30			x
239.6	Lower Granite Creek	R	30			x
239.2	Cache Creek	L	30			
238.0	Three Creeks	R	30			x
237.7	Oregon Hole	L	30			x
237.2	Upper Dry Gulch	R	30		x	x
237.0	Lower Dry Gulch	R	30	T	x	x
236.6	Hastings	R	15			
236.2	Saddle Creek	L	30	T		x
235.1	Bernard Creek	R	30	T	x	
231.6	Sluice Creek	L	30			
231.5	Rush Creek	L	30			
229.8	Johnsons Bar Landing	R	30	T	x	x
229.4	Sheep Creek	R	30	T		x
229.0	Steep Creek	R	15	T	x	
228.6	Yreka Bar	L	30	T		x
227.5	Pine Bar	R	30	T	x	x
226.5	Upper Quartz Creek	L	30	T		
226.2	Lower Quartz Creek	L	30	T	x	x
225.1	Caribou Creek	R	30	T	x	x
224.5	Dry Gulch	L	30			
224.3	Big Bar	R	30			
222.5	Upper Salt Creek	L	30	T	x	x
222.4	Lower Salt Creek	L	30	T	x	x
222.2	Two Corral	L	30	T	x	x
222.1	Gracie Bar	R	30	T	x	x

River Mile	Name	Left or Right Bank	Camp Size	Toilet	Good Landing	Shade
221.6	Half Moon Bar	R	15		x	
220.9	Slaughter Gulch	L	30	T	x	
220.3	Kirkwood Bar	R	30	T		x
220.0	Yankee Bar	L	5		x	
219.6	Russell Bar	R	30			
218.2	Cat Gulch	R	15	T	x	x
217.0	Corral Creek	R	30			x
216.4	Fish Trap Bar	L	30	T	x	
216.3	Upper Pittsburg Landing	R	30	T	x	x
216.2	Klopton Creek	R	10		x	x
215.7	Silver Shed	L	30	T	x	x
214.9	Lower Pittsburg Landing	R	30	T	x	x
213.7	Pleasant Valley	R	15			x
212.4	Davis Creek	L	10		x	
211.8	McCarty Creek	L	10			
210.8	Big Canyon	R	30	T		x
210.5	Somers Ranch	L	5			
210.4	Lower Big Canyon	R	5			
210.1	Somers Creek	L	30	T		x
209.8	Camp Creek	L	10			x
209.4	Tryon Creek	L	30	T	x	x
208.3	Lookout Creek	L	30	T	x	x
204.4	Bob Creek	L	30	T	x	x
202.9	Wolf Creek	R	5			
202.0	Bar Creek	L	30			x
199.1	Deep Creek	L	15			x
198.5	Robinson Gulch	L	30	T		x
198.3	Dug Creek	L	5			
196.6	Dug Bar Landing	L	15	T		
196.2	Dug Bar	L	15	T		
195.3	Warm Springs	R	30			x
194.1	Zig Zag	R	5		x	
193.2	Divide Creek	R	30			x
192.4	China Bar	L	30	T	x	
191.7	Imnaha	L	15	T		x
191.4	Eureka Bar	L	30	T		
190.4	Knight Creek	L	30		x	x
188.3	Salmon Mouth	R	30	T		
187.8	Salmon Bar	L	30	T		

River Mile	Name	Left or Right Bank	Camp Size	Toilet	Good Landing	Shade
184.6	Geneva Bar	L	30			
183.4	Cook Creek	L	15		x	
182.0	Lower Jim Creek	L	30	T	x	x
181.8	Meat Hole	R	5		x	
181.5	Cactus Bar	R	15	T	x	
181.1	Upper Cottonwood Creek	R	30	T	x	x
180.9	Lower Cottonwood Creek	R	30		x	x
180.2	Forest Boundary					
168.4	Public launch near Heller Bar and Confluence of Grande Ronde River					

Snake River Log

Hells Canyon Dam to Grande Ronde River

River mile: 247 to 168 .... 79 miles
Drift time: 20 hours 30 minutes .... 4.0 m.p.h.
Logged in raft
River slope: 10 feet per mile trip average
River discharge: 10,000 to 12,000 c.f.s. Hells Canyon Dam
Recommended discharge: 15,000 c.f.s. maximum
River discharge information:
    Hells Canyon Dam Discharge
    Idaho Power Company toll free recording
    1-800-422-3143-Idaho only
    1-800-521-9102 Oregon only
    Boise National Weather Service (208) 334-9860
    Monday through Friday 8:00-4:00
    Idaho river recording (208) 327-7865
    March through September
Permits and shuttle information:
    U.S. Forest Service
    Hells Canyon National Recreation Area
    2535 Riverside Drive
    P.O. Box 699
    Clarkston, WA 99403 — (509) 758-0616
    River information and permits — (509) 758-1957
Shuttle service:
    Hells Canyon Guide Service
    P. O. Box 165
    Oxbow, Oregon 97840
    Phone: (541) 785-3305, 1-800-551-7409

Wild Sheep Rapids — R.M. 241

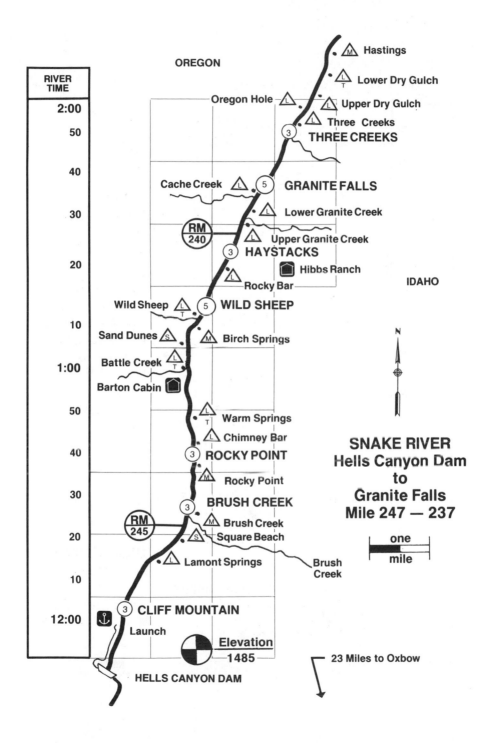

RIVER TIME

2:00
50
40
30
20
10

1:00
50
40
30
20
10

12:00

OREGON

Hastings

Lower Dry Gulch

Oregon Hole — Upper Dry Gulch

Three Creeks

THREE CREEKS

Cache Creek — GRANITE FALLS

Lower Granite Creek

RM 240 — Upper Granite Creek

HAYSTACKS

Hibbs Ranch

Rocky Bar

Wild Sheep — WILD SHEEP

IDAHO

Sand Dunes — Birch Springs

Battle Creek

Barton Cabin

Warm Springs

Chimney Bar

ROCKY POINT

Rocky Point

BRUSH CREEK

RM 245 — Brush Creek

Square Beach

Lamont Springs

Brush Creek

CLIFF MOUNTAIN

Launch

Elevation
1485

HELLS CANYON DAM

N

SNAKE RIVER
Hells Canyon Dam
to
Granite Falls
Mile 247 — 237

one
mile

23 Miles to Oxbow

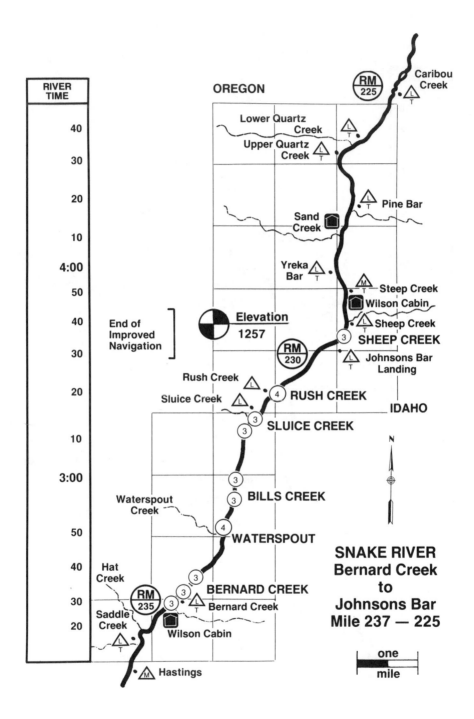

SNAKE RIVER
Bernard Creek
to
Johnsons Bar
Mile 237 — 225

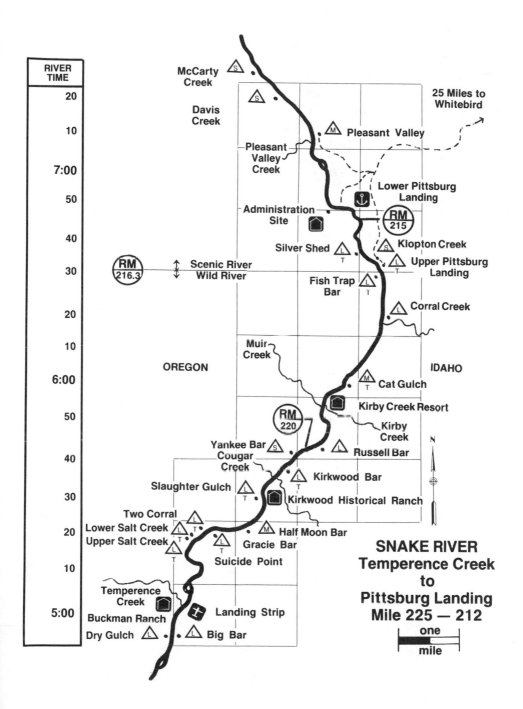

RIVER TIME

20

10

7:00

50

40

30

20

10

6:00

50

40

30

20

10

5:00

McCarty Creek

Davis Creek

Pleasant Valley

Pleasant Valley Creek

Lower Pittsburg Landing

Administration Site

RM 215

Silver Shed

Klopton Creek

Upper Pittsburg Landing

RM 216.3

Scenic River
Wild River

Fish Trap Bar

Corral Creek

Muir Creek

OREGON

IDAHO

Cat Gulch

Kirby Creek Resort

RM 220

Kirby Creek

Yankee Bar
Cougar Creek

Russell Bar

Kirkwood Bar

Slaughter Gulch

Kirkwood Historical Ranch

Two Corral

Lower Salt Creek

Upper Salt Creek

Half Moon Bar

Gracie Bar

Suicide Point

N

Temperence Creek

Buckman Ranch

Landing Strip

Dry Gulch

Big Bar

25 Miles to Whitebird

SNAKE RIVER
Temperence Creek
to
Pittsburg Landing
Mile 225 — 212

one
mile

257

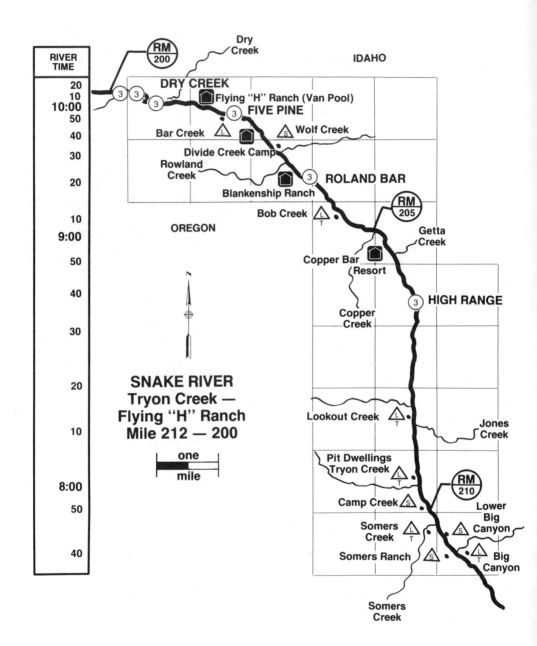

SNAKE RIVER
Tryon Creek —
Flying "H" Ranch
Mile 212 — 200

258

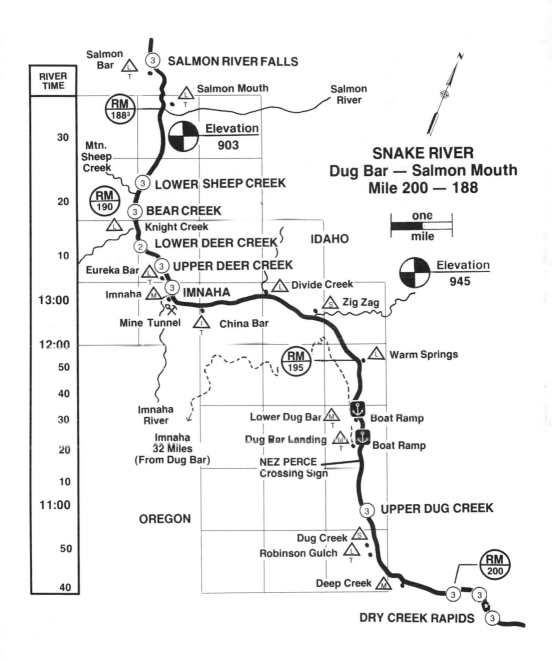

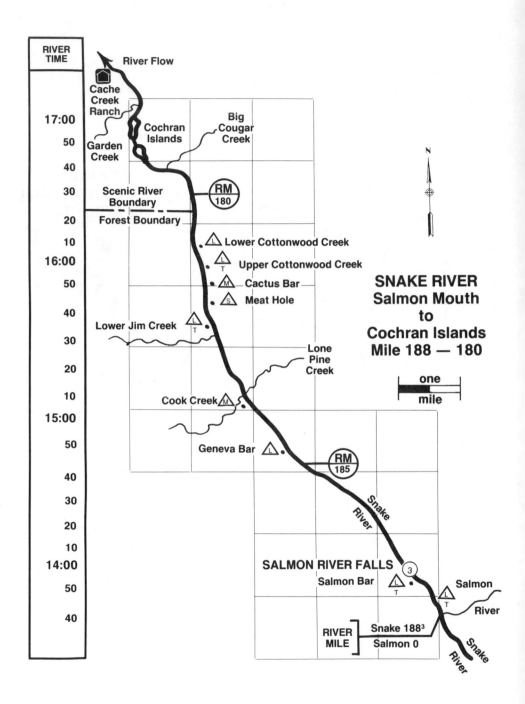

RIVER
TIME

River Flow

Cache
Creek
Ranch

17:00

50

Cochran
Islands

Big
Cougar
Creek

40

Garden
Creek

30

Scenic River
Boundary

RM
180

20

Forest Boundary

10

Lower Cottonwood Creek

16:00

Upper Cottonwood Creek

50

Cactus Bar

40

Meat Hole

Lower Jim Creek

30

Lone
Pine
Creek

20

10

Cook Creek

15:00

50

Geneva Bar

RM
185

40

30

Snake
River

20

10

14:00

SALMON RIVER FALLS

3

50

Salmon Bar

Salmon

40

River

RIVER
MILE

Snake 188³

Salmon 0

Snake
River

SNAKE RIVER
Salmon Mouth
to
Cochran Islands
Mile 188 — 180

one
mile

N

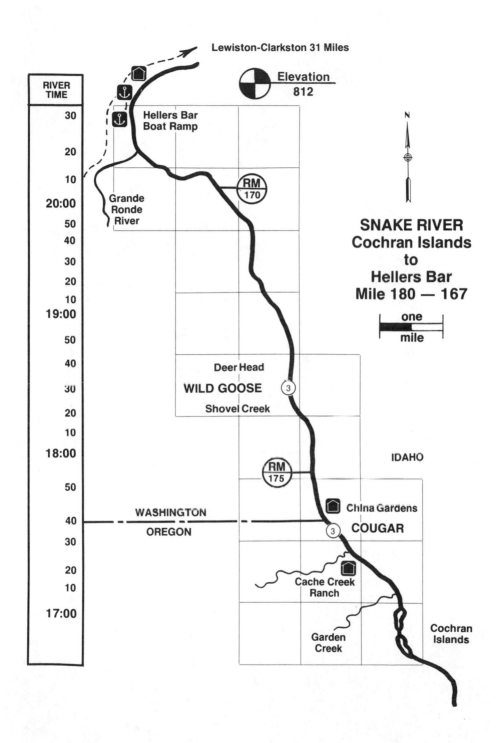

Lewiston-Clarkston 31 Miles

RIVER TIME

Elevation
812

Hellers Bar
Boat Ramp

30

20

10

20:00

Grande
Ronde
River

N

SNAKE RIVER
Cochran Islands
to
Hellers Bar
Mile 180 — 167

one
mile

50

40

30

20

10

19:00

50

40

30

20

10

18:00

Deer Head

WILD GOOSE

Shovel Creek

RM
170

RM
175

3

IDAHO

50

40

30

20

10

17:00

WASHINGTON

OREGON

China Gardens

COUGAR

3

Cache Creek
Ranch

Garden
Creek

Cochran
Islands

261

North Umpqua River — R.M. 66

North Umpqua River

Boulder Flat to Gravel Bin

The North Umpqua River has its origins near Diamond Lake. It flows 106 miles to meet the South Umpqua River, continuing as the main Umpqua River for another 112 miles to the Pacific Ocean at Reedsport. The Umpqua River and its tributaries present Oregonians a complex pattern of waterways for boating, fishing, and general recreation. The North Umpqua River near Steamboat Creek has long been recognized as a premier fishery, attracting notables such as Zane Grey from all over. Only within the last few years, coincident with the whitewater boom, has this river also achieved recognition as one of Oregon's most popular whitewater rivers. The river has recently been included in both State and Federal legislation under the State Scenic Waterways and the Federal Wild and Scenic Rivers Acts.

The section of the river from Boulder Flat Campground to the gravel bin launch near Steamboat Creek is considered by boaters to be the best whitewater boating in the entire Umpqua River basin. This section, in spite of its reputation as both a premier fishing and whitewater boating section, avoids the fisher-boater conflicts encountered downstream from Steamboat Creek. The section described in this log is boatable almost the entire year within the recommended river flows between 1,000-2,000 c.f.s. Within this range of flow the river is regarded as a class three-four river difficulty One of the most notable rapids in this section is Pinball, which illustrates the maximum rapids difficulty of this tour. To scout Pinball before going on the river, walk 0.4 mile downstream on the road from the Apple Creek bridge to the landmark osprey nest, then 85 yards further to a short, steep, inconspicuous poison-oak lined trail from the road near road mile 43. The trail leads to a bluff overlooking Pinball Rapids. Boaters who do not want to run Pinball exit at the Apple Creek Camp just before the Apple Creek bridge. Boaters continuing through Pinball can see the osprey nest from the river and, at low water, can scout on the left bank near a gravel bar just before Pinball. At flows of 4,000 c.f.s. and greater the rocks at this rapids are mostly covered and at lower flows they become more evident and trouble-some. Scout Pinball and draw your own conclusions.

River flows for the North Umpqua are not a normal part of the National Weather Service recording. Flows can be obtained from the National Weather Service for the Winchester gage, which is over 50 miles downstream from this tour. Information on a gage near Glide (R.M. 48) can be obtained Monday through Friday from Douglas

County Water Resources (541) 440-4255. Local boaters use the Copeland Creek gage at road mile 51.4 which has easy access from the road enroute to the Boulder Flat launch. At gage readings above 7.0 feet (2,340 c.f.s.) the river is bank to bank, and the normally clear blue-green water turns to gray-green. At a 9.0 gage (4,800 c.f.s.), or above, the river is brown and considered to be at flood stage. At the flows normally boated, between 1,000-2,000 c.f.s., the river channel becomes more defined. The pool and drop character of the river is more evident in the rocky channel where the manuevering becomes quite precise and technical.

The North Umpqua is a small, emerald green, mist shrouded, old growth fur lined canyon. There are nice camps which more than compensate for the paralleling road and its constant stream of log trucks. This is one of the best whitewater day trips in Oregon, and it can be extended to an overnight trip by using the convenient camps.

North Umpqua River Log

Boulder Flat to Gravel Bin

River mile: 68 to 54 .... 14 miles
Drift time: 3 hours 30 minutes .... 4 m.p.h.
Logged in raft
River slope: 32 feet per mile average
River discharge: 1,020 c.f.s. 5.4 feet Copeland Creek gage.
Recommended discharge: 1,000 - 2,000 c.f.s.
River discharge information:
    Local boaters use Copeland gage which is not available from National Weather Service.
Information:
    Managed by Umpqua National Forest
    P. O. Box 1008
    Roseburg, OR 97470
    (541) 672-6601
Shuttle:
    Cimarron Outdoors, Inc.
    North Umpqua Highway 138
    Box 62
    Idleyld Park, OR 97447
    (541) 498-2235

NORTH UMPQUA RIVER

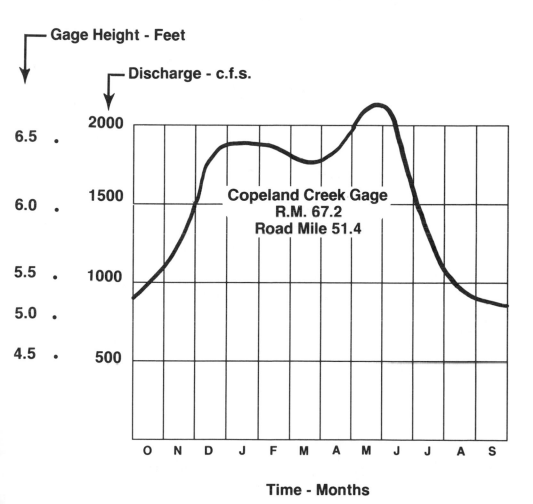

Gage Height - Feet

Discharge - c.f.s.

Copeland Creek Gage
R.M. 67.2
Road Mile 51.4

O N D J F M A M J J A S

Time - Months

RIVER MILE	RIVER TIME	LEFT BANK	RAPIDS	RIGHT BANK	DESCRIPTION
RM 60	2:00			⛺	Islands
	55		⊙⊙ 2		
	50		2	⛺	
	45		>2		
	40		3		
	35		3 ⊟ 2	⛺	Double ledges Horseshoe Bend Bridge
	30		3 ⊙		Boulder Island
	25		3 2		
	20		3	〜〜	Dry Creek
	15		2		
	10		3		
	5		>2		
	1:00	〜〜	2		Deception Creek
	55				
	50	⊙	2 2		Island
	45				
RM 65	40		2 ⊟ 2 2		Marster Bridge
	35				
	30		⊙		Island
	25				
	20	⊟ 〜	>2		Copeland Creek
	15	⌂			Gage house left
	10		2 3	〜〜	Boulder Creek
	05		3		
	12:00	⛺ ⚓	3		Boulder Flat camp and launch

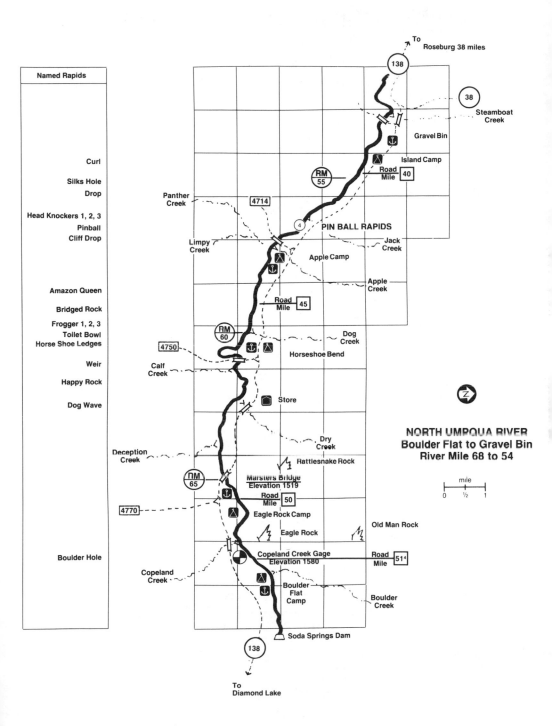

Named Rapids

Curl

Silks Hole

Drop

Head Knockers 1, 2, 3
Pinball
Cliff Drop

Amazon Queen

Bridged Rock

Frogger 1, 2, 3
Toilet Bowl
Horse Shoe Ledges

Weir

Happy Rock

Dog Wave

Deception
Creek

Boulder Hole

To
Roseburg 38 miles

138

38
Steamboat
Creek

Gravel Bin

Island Camp

RM
55

Road
Mile 40

Panther
Creek

4714

4
PIN BALL RAPIDS

Jack
Creek

Limpy
Creek

Apple Camp

Apple
Creek

Road
Mile 45

RM
60

Dog
Creek

4750

Horseshoe Bend

Calf
Creek

Store

Dry
Creek

NORTH UMPQUA RIVER
Boulder Flat to Gravel Bin
River Mile 68 to 54

Rattlesnake Rock

Marsters Bridge
Elevation 1519

RM
65

Road
Mile 50

4770

Eagle Rock Camp

Old Man Rock

Eagle Rock

Copeland Creek Gage
Elevation 1580

Road
Mile 51⁴

Copeland
Creek

Boulder
Flat
Camp

Boulder
Creek

mile
0   ½   1

Soda Springs Dam

138

To
Diamond Lake

RIVER MILE	RIVER TIME	LEFT BANK	RAPIDS	RIGHT BANK	DESCRIPTION
	4:00				
	55				
	50				
RM 53	45				
	40				
	35				
	30			⚓	Gravel Bin takeout
	25			⛺	Island Camp
	20		• 2		
RM 55	15		• 2		
	10				
	05		• 2		
			• 2		
	3:00		• 2		
	55				PINBALL Scout
	50		4 •		
	45			⛺	Apple Bridge Apple Camp Island
	40				
	35				
	30		3 • / • 2		
	25		3 • / • 2 / • 2 / • 2		
	20				
	15		3 • / • 2		Islands Log Over Channel
	10		3 • / • 2	∿∿∿	Waterfall right bank
	05		3 • / • 2 / • 2		
RM 60	2:00		3 • / • 2		

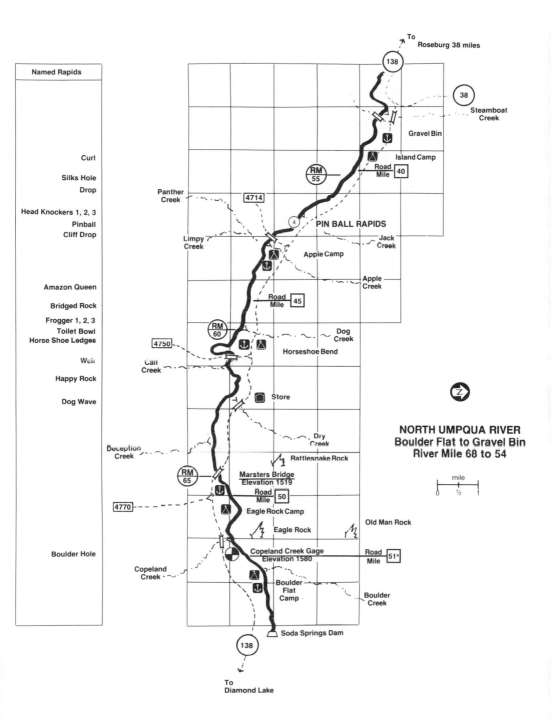

Named Rapids

Curl

Silks Hole

Drop

Head Knockers 1, 2, 3
Pinball
Cliff Drop

Amazon Queen

Bridged Rock

Frogger 1, 2, 3
Toilet Bowl
Horse Shoe Ledges

Weir

Happy Rock

Dog Wave

Boulder Hole

To
Roseburg 38 miles

138

38

Steamboat
Creek

Gravel Bin

Island Camp

RM 55

Road Mile 40

Panther
Creek

4714

4 PIN BALL RAPIDS

Jack
Creek

Limpy
Creek

Apple Camp

Apple
Creek

Road Mile 45

RM 60

Dog
Creek

4750

Horseshoe Bend

Carr
Creek

Store

Dry
Creek

Deception
Creek

Rattlesnake Rock

RM 65

Marsters Bridge
Elevation 1519

Road Mile 50

4770

Eagle Rock Camp

Eagle Rock

Old Man Rock

Copeland Creek Gage
Elevation 1580

Road Mile 51⁴

Copeland
Creek

Boulder
Flat
Camp

Boulder
Creek

Soda Springs Dam

138

To
Diamond Lake

**NORTH UMPQUA RIVER
Boulder Flat to Gravel Bin
River Mile 68 to 54**

mile
0 ½ 1

References

1. *Idaho River Tours* by Garren. Includes Hells Canyon of the Snake River.

2. *Handbook to the Rogue River* by Quinn, Quinn.

3. *Handbook to the Illinois River* by Quinn, Quinn.

4. *Handbook to the Deschutes River* by Quinn, Quinn.

5. *Hells Corner Gorge of the Upper Klamath* Quinn Map.

6. Snake River of Hells Canyon by Carrey and Conley.

7. *Soggy Sneakers Guide to Oregon Rivers* by Willamette Kayak and Canoe Club.

8. John Day River by Campbell.

9. The Wild and Scenic Snake River. River maps by Hells Canyon Natural Recreation Area.

10. *Canoe Routes — Northwest Oregon* by Jones.

11. *Oregon's Quiet Waters* by McLean and Brown.

12. *Washington Whitewater 2*, by Douglas A. North.

13. Rogue River Float Guide. Available from USFS or BLM.